George Du Maurier,

A legend of Camelot : pictures and poems, etc.

George Du Maurier, publisher Harper & Brothers
A legend of Camelot : pictures and poems, etc.
ISBN/EAN: 9783337628734
Printed in Europe, USA, Canada, Australia, Japan
Cover: Foto ©ninafisch / pixelio.de

More available books at **www.hansebooks.com**

A Legend of Camelot, &c.

A Legend of Camelot,

Pictures and Poems,

ETC.

By George du Maurier.

NEW YORK AND LONDON:
HARPER AND BROTHERS, PUBLISHERS.

INTRODUCTION.

THE "Legend of Camelot," with the other Poems and Pictures, &c., which make up the present Volume, originally appeared in the pages of *Punch*, with the exception of the Poem entitled "A Lost Illusion." This was printed in the "Recreations of the Rabelais Club," issued for private circulation, and was there illustrated by a reduced extract (with slight variation) from the Picture now given.

October, 1897.

CONTENTS.

	FOLIO
A LEGEND OF CAMELOT	1
FLIRTS IN HADES	13
POOR PUSSY'S NIGHTMARE	14
THE CONTRAST	16
THE FOOLS' PARADISE	18
A LOST ILLUSION	20
VERS NONSENSIQUES	24
L'ONGLAY À PARRY	41
TWO THRONES	45

CONTENTS—*Continued.*

	FOLIO
A LOVE-AGONY	47
A SIMPLE STORY	49
A BALLAD OF BLUNDERS	53
THE RISE AND FALL OF THE JACK SPRATTS	56
A MODEL HERO OF MODERN ROMANCE	91

A Legend of Camelot.

Part 1.

ALL Braunighrindas left her bed
At cock-crow with an aching head.
    ☞ misrrir!

"I yearn to suffer and to do,"
She cried, "ere sunset, something new!
    ☞ misrrir!

To do and suffer, ere I die,
I care not what. I know not why.
    ☞ misrrir!

Some quest I crave to undertake,
Or burden bear, or trouble make."
    ☞ misrrir!

She shook her hair about her form
In waves of colour bright and warm.
    ☞ misrrir!

It rolled and writhed, and reached the floor:
A silver wedding-ring she wore.
    ☞ misrrir!

She left her tower, and wandered down
Into the High Street of the town.
    ☞ misrrir!

Her pale feet glimmered, in and out,
Like tombstones as she went about.
    ☞ misrrir!

From right to left, and left to right;
And blue veins streakt her insteps white;
    ☞ misrrir!

And folks did ask her in the street
"How fared it with her long pale feet?"
    ☞ misrrir!

And blinkt, as though 'twere hard to bear
The red-heat of her blazing hair!
    ☞ misrrir!

Sir Galahad and Sir Launcelot
Came hand-in-hand down Camelot;
    ☞ misrrir!

Sir Gauwaine followed close behind;
A weight hung heavy on his mind.
    ☞ misrrir!

"Who knows this damsel, burning bright,"
Quoth Launcelot, "like a northern light"?
    ☞ misrrir!

Quoth Sir Gauwaine: *"I know her not!"*
"Who quoth you did?" quoth Launcelot.
    ☞ misrrir!

"'Tis Braunighrindas!" quoth Sir Bors.
(Just then returning from the wars.)
    ☞ misrrir!

Then quoth the pure Sir Galahad:
"She seems, methinks, but lightly clad!
    ☞ misrrir!

The winds blow somewhat chill to-day.
Moreover, what would Arthur say!"
    ☞ misrrir!

She thrust her chin towards Galahad
Full many an inch beyond her head. . . .
    ☞ misrrir!

But when she noted Sir Gauwaine
She wept, and drew it in again!
    ☞ misrrir!

She wept: "How beautiful am I!"
He shook the poplars with a sigh.
    ☞ misrrir!

Sir Launcelot was standing near;
Him kist he thrice behind the ear.
    ☞ misrrir!

"Ah me!" sighed Launcelot where he stood,
"I cannot fathom it!" . . . (who could?)
    ☞ misrrir!

Hard by his wares a weaver wove,
And weaving with a will, he throve;
    ☞ misrrir!

Him beckoned Galahad, and said,—
"Gaunt Braunighrindas wants your aid . . . .
    ☞ misrrir!

Behold the wild growth from her nape!
Good weaver, weave it into shape!"
    ☞ misrrir!

The weaver wove the wild waste room;
Did lead her, whilst the knights made room;
    ☞ misrrir!

And wove her locks, both web and woof,
And made them wind and waterproof;
    ☞ misrrir!

Then with his shears he opened wide
An arm-hole neat on either side,
    ☞ misrrir!

And bound her with his handkerchief
Right round the middle like a sheaf.
    ☞ misrrir!

"Are you content, knight?" quoth Sir Bors
To Galahad; quoth he, "Of course!"
    ☞ misrrir!

"Ah, me! those locks," quoth Sir Gauwaine,
"Will never know the comb again!"
    ☞ misrrir!

The bold Sir Launcelot quoth he nought;
So (haply) all the more he thought.
    ☞ misrrir!

"Behold the wild growth from her nape."

Part 2.

AN one-eyed Eastern past, who sold,
And bought, and bartered garments old;
A triple head-dress crowned his head ;
His yellow garb did show the thread,
    O misrtir!

And, ever and anon, his throat,
Thick-bearded, gave a solemn note ;
    O misrtir!

The knights were gathered in a knot;
Rapt in a trance, they heard him not ;
    O misrtir!

Before them Braunighrindas stood
In native growth of gown and hood ;
    O misrtir!

Fresh from a cunning weaver's hand,
She lookt, not gaudy, but so grand !
    O misrtir!

Not gaudy, gentles, but so neat !
For chaste and knightly eyes a treat !
    O misrtir!

The Pilgrim eyed her shapely dress
With curious eye to business :
    O misrtir!

Then whispered he to Launcelot,
" I'll give five shekels for the lot !"
    O misrtir!

Gauwaine his battle-axe he drew . . . .
Once and again he clove him through !
    O misrtir!

" No man of many words am I !"
Quoth he, and wope his weapon dry.
    O misrtir!

A butcher caught the sounds and said,
" There go two cracks upon one head !"
    O misrtir!

A baker whispered in his fun :
" Butcher, more heads are crackt than one !"
    O misrtir!

" The moon is up to many tricks !"
Quoth he who made the candlesticks ! . . . .
    O misrtir!

Dead-limp, the unbeliever lay
Athwart the flags and stopt the way. . . . .
    O misrtir!

The bold Sir Launcelot mused a bit,
And smole a bitter smile at it.
    O misrtir!

Gauwaine, he gave his orders brief :—
" *Manants : emportez-moi ce Juif !* "
    O misrtir!

Some heard the knight not : they that heard
Made answer to him none, nor stirred.
    O misrtir

But Braunighrindas was not dumb ;
Her opportunity had come.
    O misrtir!

Her accents tinkled ivory-sweet—
" *Je vays l'importer tout de suite !*" . . . .
    O misrtir!

She bowed her body, slenderly,
And lifted him full tenderly ;
    O misrtir!

Full silverly her stretched throat
Intoned the wonted Hebrew note :
    O misrtir!

Right broke-in-halfenly she bent ;
Jew-laden on her way she went !
    O misrtir!

. The knights all left her one by one,
And, leaving, cried in unison—
    O misrtir!

" *Voyez ce vilain Juif qui pend
Par derrière et par devant !* ". . .
    O misrtir!

Yet bearing it she journeyed forth,
Selecting north-north-east by north.
    O misrtir!

The knights (most wisely) with one mouth,
Selected south-south-west by south.
    O misrtir!

The butcher, baker, and the rest,
Said, " Let them go where they like best !"
    O misrtir!

And many a wink they wunk, and shook
Their heads ; but furthermore they took
    O misrtir!

No note : it was a way they had,
In Camelot, when folks went mad. . . . .
    O misrtir!

"Fez-laden on her way she went."

Part 3.

SHE bore her burden all that day
Half-faint; the unconverted clay
  Half-faint;
    O misrtir!

A burden grew, beneath the sun,
In many a manner more than one.
    O misrtir!

Half-faint the whitening road along
She bore it, singing (in her song)—
    O misrtir!

"The locks you loved, Gauwaine, Gauwaine,
Will never know the comb again! . . .
The man you slew, Gauwaine, Gauwaine,
Will never come to life again!
So when they do, Gauwaine, Gauwaine,
Then take me back to town again!"
    O misrtir!

The shepherds gazed, but marvelled not;
They knew the ways of Camelot!
    O misrtir!

She heeded neither man nor beast:
Her shadow lengthened toward the east.
    O misrtir!

A little castle she drew nigh,
With seven towers twelve inches high. . . .
    O misrtir!

A baby castle, all a-flame
With many a flower that hath no name.
    O misrtir!

It had a little moat all round;
A little drawbridge too she found,
    O misrtir!

On which there stood a stately maid,
Like her in radiant locks arrayed . . .
    O misrtir!

Save that her locks grew rank and wild,
By weaver's shuttle undefiled! . . .
    O misrtir!

Who held her brush and comb, as if
Her faltering hands had waxéd stiff
    O misrtir!

With baulkt endeavour! whence she sung
A chant, the burden whereof rung:
    O misrtir!

"These hands have striven in vain
    To part
  These locks that won Gauwaine
    His heart!"

All breathless, Braunghrindas stopt
To listen, and her load she dropt,
    O misrtir!

And rolled in wonder wild and blear
The whites of her eyes grown green with fear:
    O misrtir!

"What is your name, young person, pray?"
"Knights call me Fidele-strynges-le-Fay."
    O misrtir!

"You wear a wedding-ring, I see!"
"I do . . . Gauwaine he gave it me". . . .
    O misrtir!

"Are you Gauwaine his wedded spouse?
Is this Gauwaine his . . . country-house?"
    O misrtir!

—"I am . . . it is . . . we are . . . oh who,
That you should greet me thus, are you?"
    O misrtir!

—"I am ANOTHER! . . . since the morn
The fourth month of the year was born!". . .
    O misrtir!

—"What! that which followed when the last
Bleak night of bitter March had past?" . . . .
    O misrtir!

—"The same." —"That day for both hath done!
And you, and he, and I, are ONE!" . . . .
    O misrtir!

Then hand in hand, most woefully,
They went, the willows weeping nigh;
    O misrtir!

Left hand in left was left to cling!
On each a silver wedding-ring.
    O misrtir!

And having walkt a little space,
They halted, each one in her place:
    O misrtir!

And chanted loud a wondrous plaint
Well chosen: wild, one-noted, quaint:
    O misrtir!

"Heigho! the Wind and the Rain!
  The Moon's at the Full, Gauwaine, Gauwaine
Heigho! the Wind and the Rain
  On gold-hair woven, and gold-hair plain!
Heigho! the Wind and the Rain!
  Oh when shall we Three meet again!"

Atween the river and the wood,
Knee-deep 'mid whispering reeds they stood:
    O misrtir!

The green earth oozing soft and dank
Beneath them, soakt and suckt and sank! . . . .
    O misrtir!

Yet soak-and-suck-and-sink or not,
They, chanting, craned towards Camelot. . . .
    O misrtir!

"On which there stood a stately maid."

Part 4.

THE pale wet moon did rise and ride,
O'er misty wolds and marshes wide.
　O miserie!

Sad earth slept underneath the yew,
Lapt in the death-sweat men call dew.
　O miserie!

O raven ringlets, ringing wet!
O bright eye rolling black as jet!
　O miserie!

O matted locks about the chin!
O towering head-piece, battered in!
　O miserie!

Three hats that fit each other tight,
Are worth the helmet of a knight!
　O miserie!

He rose all shapeless from the mud,
His yellow garb was stained with blood;
　O miserie!

"Vat ish thish schwimming in mine head?
Thish turning round and round?" he said.
　O miserie!

He took three paces through the night,
He saw red gold that glittered bright!
　O miserie!

Two Royal Heads of Hair he saw!
And One was Woven, and One was Raw!
　O miserie!

"O Sholomon! if there ain't a pair
Of dead young damshels shinking there!
　O miserie!

O Moshesh! vat a precioush lot
Of beautiful red hair they've got!
　O miserie!

The prishe of it would compenshate
Most handshome for my broken pate!
　O miserie!

How much their upper lipsh do pout!
How very much their chins shtick out!
　O miserie!

How dreadful shtrange they shtare! they sheen
Half to be dead, and half to dream!
　O miserie!

The Camelot peoplesh alvaysh try
To look like that! I yonder vy?
　O miserie!

Yet each hath got a lovely fashe!
Good Father Jacob shend them grashe!
　O miserie!

O Jacob! blesh the lovely light,
That lit the moon that shtruck the knight,
That married the maid that carried the Jew,
That shold (as he intensh to do)
The golden locks and shilver rings
Of Braunighrinde and Fiddleshtrings!"
　O miserie!

Thus having given thanks, he drew
His two-fold weapon cutting true;
　O miserie!

And close the clipt, and clean and clear,
From crown and temple, nape and ear.
　O miserie!

The wind in pity soughed and sighed!
The river beat the river side!
　O miserie!

The willows wept to stand and see
The sweetest, softest heads that be,
　O miserie!

In ghastliest baldness gleam dead-white,
And sink unhallowed out of sight!
　O miserie!

But, lo, you! Ere kind earth could fold
Their shame within its bosom cold,
　O miserie!

*The moon lud laught in mockery down,
And stampt a high-light on each crown!!* ..

Thrice muttering deep his mystic note,
The stillness of the night he smote:
　O miserie!

Then, with a treasure dangling slack
From either shoulder adown his back,
　O miserie!

He, whistling in his whistle, strode,
Nor felt he faint upon the road!
　O miserie!

You may be sure that it was not
The road that leads to Camelot!
　O miserie!

"*Two Royal Heads of Hair he saw.*"

Part 3.

THE castle weeds have grown so tall
Knights cannot see the red brick wall.
    O miseris!

The little drawbridge hangs awry,
The little flowery moat is dry!
    O miseris!

And the wind, it soughs and sighs alway
Through the grey willows, night and day!
    O miseris!

And evermore two willows there
Do weep, whose boughs are always bare:
    O miseris!

At all times weep they, in and out
Of season, turn and turn about!
    O miseris!

But later, when the year doth fall,
And other willows, one and all,
    O miseris!

In yellowing and dishevelled leaf
Sway haggard with their autumn grief,
    O miseris!

Then do these leafless willows now
Put forth a rosebud from each bough!
    O miseris!

What time Gauwaine, with spurless heels,
Barefoot (but not bare-headed) kneels
    O miseris!

Between! . . . as fits a bigamous knight
Twice widowed in a single night:
    O miseris!

And then, for that promiscuous way
Of axing Hebrews in broad day,
    O miseris!

He ever uttereth a note
Of Eastern origin remote. . . .
    O miseris!

A well-known monochord, that tells
Of one who, wandering, buys and sells!
    O miseris!

What time the knights and damsels fair
Of Arthur's court come trooping there,
    O miseris!

They come in dresses of dark green,
Two damsels take a knight between:
    O miseris!

One sad and sallow knight is fixt
Dyspeptic damsels twain betwixt!
    O miseris!

They speak not, but their weary eyes
And wan white eyelids droop and rise
    O miseris!

With dim dead gaze of mystic woe!
They always take their pleasure so
    O miseris!

In Camelot. . . . It doth not lie
With us to ask, or answer, why!
    O miseris!

Yet, seeing them so fair and good,
Fain would we cheer them, if we could!
    O miseris!

And every time they find a bud,
They pluck it, and it bleeds red blood.
    O miseris!

And when they pluck a full-blown rose,
And breathe the same, its colour goes!
    O miseris!

But with Gauwaine alone at night,
The willows dance in their delight!
    O miseris!

The rosebuds wriggle in their bliss,
And lift them for his lips to kiss!
    O miseris!

And if he kiss a rose instead,
It blushes of a deeper red!
    O miseris!

And if he like it, let him be!
It makes no odds to you or me!
    O miseris!

O many-headed multitude,
Who read these rhymes that run so rude,
    O miseris!

Strive not to fathom their intent!
But say your prayers, and rest content
    O miseris!

That, notwithstanding those two cracks
He got from Gauwaine's battle-axe,
    O miseris!

The Hebrew had the best of it!
So, Gentles, let us rest a bit.
    O miseris!

"Two damsels take a Knight between."

Verses and Sketches.

FLIRTS IN HADES.

YE maids, that practise wicked arts,
And eke young widows with light hearts;
Gay Guardsmen, and pet parsons dear,
And all such heartbreakers, see here!
I charge you all, and every one,
To waste no love ye may have won,
For fear of this grey limbo, where
All you fine flirts that ever were
Of either sex, shall bud and blow
As grafts on rooted stems, and grow,
For many a round of days and years,
Self-watered with your own salt tears;
And wipe your eyes on your own leaves,
For lack of pocket-handkerchieves!
And wet your lips at your own cost,
To whistle for the loves you lost;
That these may cast their eyes, and see
Fit cause to kiss, and set you free;
For if by dint of tears, or trace
Of some old unforgotten grace,

You chance to charm a stray kiss out
Of lips you once were fain to flout,
Then may you pluck yourselves, and use
Your leaves for pinions, if you choose,
To soar upon, and seek for peace;
Thus, only thus, the spell shall cease.
And trust me, you shall not, I trow,
Be beautiful and bright, as now;
Your features shall be modelled then
By Mr. Punch's smart young men!
And here your victims, great and small,
Shall whisk about you, one and all;
With banded wings like butterflies,
And, oh! such beautiful big eyes!
And eyelashes an inch at least,
And all their wealth of locks increast!
And faces brighter than of old,
And beautified a billion-fold,
And little else but face to show,
For having buried long ago

Their bodies, and the broken hearts
That plagued them so, in foreign parts;
In fact, such faces as you see
In keepsakes gilded gorgeously!
And they shall have sweet kisses too,
But none to waste on such as you!
No! they shall either cut you dead,
Or take to teasing you instead,
And point at you, and poke their fun,
And try your tempers, one by one,
And raise false hopes and lay them low,
And pout their lips to kiss, and go!
So shall they nip you in the bud,
Or leave you sticking in the mud,
That you may rue your fickle days
Of dancing, and your jilting ways!
Till haply you shall culminate
In quite a vegetable state,
And even run to waste, I wis,
And all for want of one poor kiss!

POOR PUSSY'S NIGHTMARE.

ALL on a bare and bleak hillside,
One night this merry Christmas-tide,
A shivering, hunted hare did hide—
    Poor Pussy!

Though we had hunted Puss all day,
The wind had blown her scent away,
And baulked the dogs—so there she lay,
    Did Pussy!

There to the earth she humbly crept—
There, brooding o'er her lot, she wept—
There, on her empty stomach, slept
    Poor Pussy!

And there, whilst fell the frozen dew,
She dreamt an ugly dream or two,
As starved wet folk are apt to do,
    Did Pussy.

Loud hungry hounds of subtle ken,
And thundering steeds, and hard-eyed men,
Are fast on Pussy's trail again—
    Poor Pussy!

Onward she strains—on, on they tear!
Foremost amongst the foremost there
Are ruthless women's faces fair!
    Poor Pussy!

One moment's check! To left—to right—
In vain she spends her little might!
Some yokel's eye has marked her flight—
    Poor Pussy!

What use her five small wits to rack?
Closer and faster on her track
Hurries the hydra-headed pack!
    Lost Pussy!

"For pity's sake, kind huntsman, stop!
Call off the dogs, before I drop,
And kill me with your heavy crop!"
    Shrieks Pussy!

With shuddering start and stifled scream,
She wakes—she finds it all a dream!
How kind the cold, cold earth doth seem
    To Pussy!

In harrying Puss we had great fun,
And trust that ere this year be done
She'll give us yet one other run,
    Will Pussy!

A softer wind, a cloudier sky,
A nice damp turf for the scent to lie,
Are all we ask! Till then, good-bye,
    Dear Pussy!

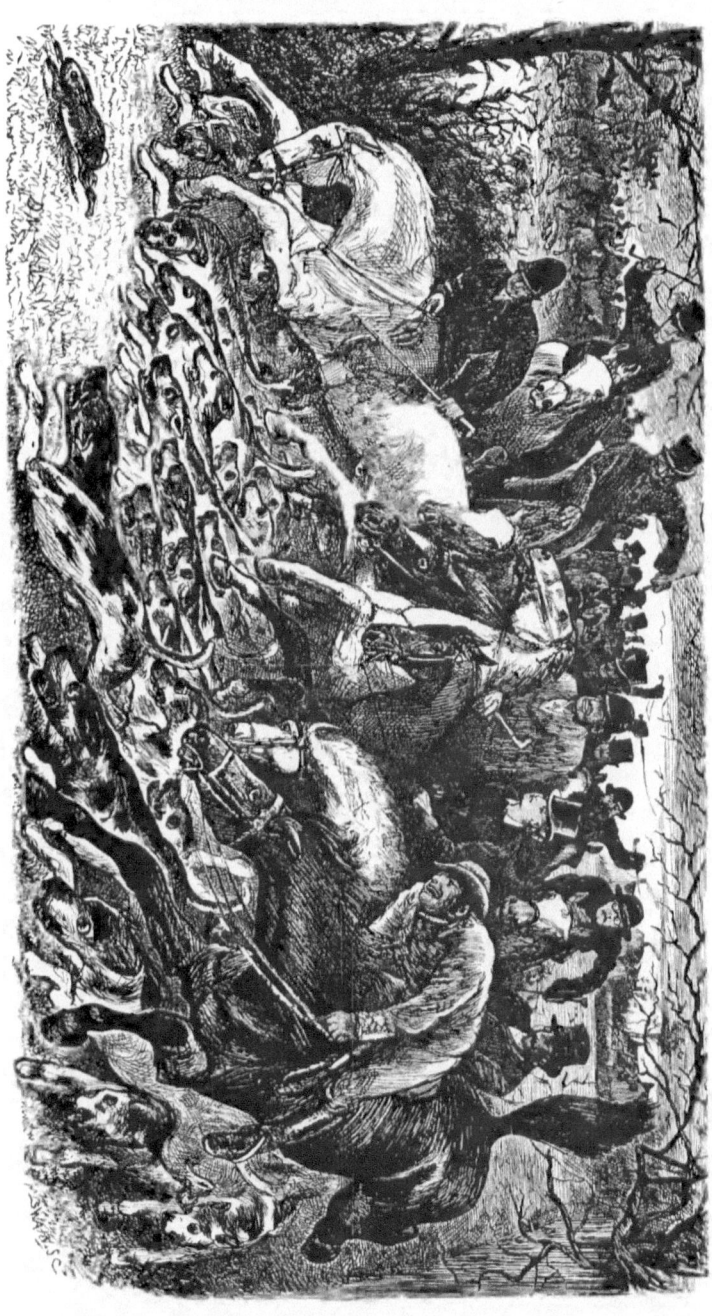

"Onward they stream—on, on they tear!"

THE CONTRAST.

At a Sale of Antique Furniture.

WHEN the mirror politely stood still for a space,
And she viewed herself there in that reeking old place,
While the tribes clustered, grinning, all round her sweet face,
Such a picture was framed as one don't often see;

    On our Catalogue's margin we sketched her, *pro tem.*,
    And just added those lively descendants of Shem
    For a background—the brighter and fairer the gem,
    The darker and plainer the setting should be!

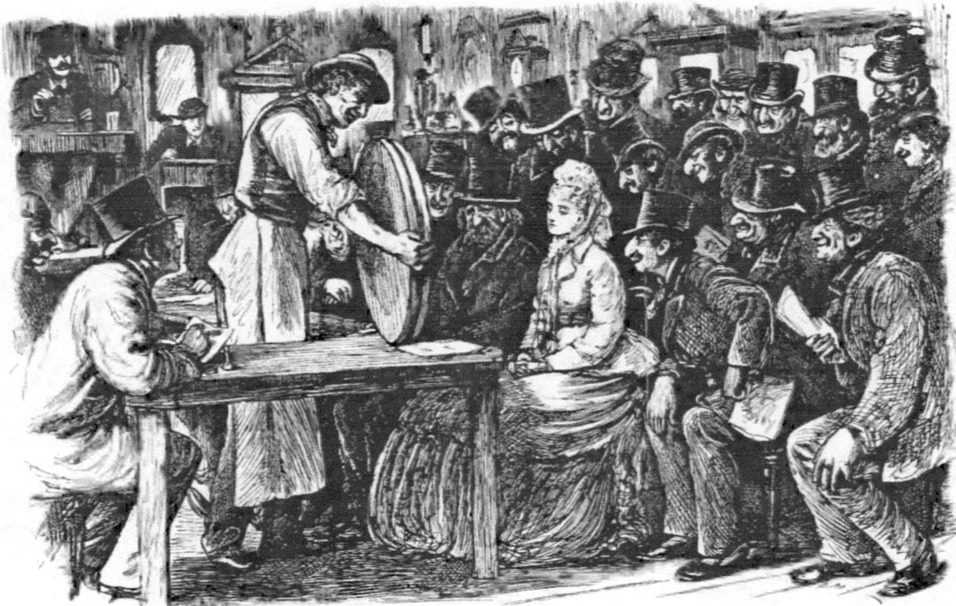

"And she viewed herself there."

"Take up your chain together."

THE FOOLS' PARADISE.

I.

IN and about the Honeymoon,
  Young Love in his fever groweth;
He waxeth fast, he waneth soon,
  He cometh, and he goeth.
Young Love hath wings that flout his legs,
  And soareth, Life unheeding;
Young Love is the goose with the golden
    Eggs!
And soon he lies a-bleeding!

II.

The road is red with roses sweet,
  That leads you to his Dwelling
With shoes of swiftness on your feet,
  And Joy there is no telling!
And each a cap about the brow,
  But ne'er the Cap of Knowledge:
The Cap of many Bells I trow,
  Fits best in Young Love's College!

III.

He weaves his bandage round your
    eyes,
  He casts his blindness o'er you,
That you may dream all Paradise
  Doth stretch away before you!
And dreaming each the other blest
  With Love's own wings behind you,
You dare the Parson do his best
  For aye and a day to bind you!

IV.

For all a month He bids you fain
  Go feed among the Posies;
And hides the Padlock and the Chain
  For all a Month of Roses;
And gives you nought to care about
  But Love, till Truth be minded
That you should find each other out,
  And be no longer blinded!

V.

O Love! that all the best of you
  Be over with the wooing!
O Wedlock! All the worst of you
  That there be no undoing!
It's Hey! Ho! and Welladay
  For Youth and Love, and Honey!
It's Heigho! and Workaday
  For Bread and Cheese, and Money!

VI.

Weep not, poor Fools, nor hold aloof!
  Take up your chain together,
And earthwards pad the wandering hoof
  That brought you fooling hither!
O Help each other, and share the load,
  For steep the pass and thorny,
That leads you thorough from Love's
    Abode
To Life, and rough the Journey!

VII.

"—O Dream of Dreams! O was it worth
  The pain of this our waking?
O what is there of balm on earth
  Can heal us of our aching?
O Love is he dead before the Prime,
  Love that was born so newly?" . . .
—Poor Fools, go pin your faith on Time,
  And Time shall tell you duly.

VIII.

For Time that scorned Love's earlier
    ways,
  His mellower secrets holdeth;
These, living out our length of Days,
  We learn as Truth unfoldeth.
Who knows but in a year or two
  That Love may have the kindness
To come without his wings to you,
  And holpen of his blindness?

A LOST ILLUSION.

I.

THERE was a young woman, and what do you think?
  She lived upon nothing but paper and ink!
For ink and for paper she only did care,
Though they wrinkle the forehead and rumple the hair.

II.

And she bought a gold pen, and she plied it so fast
  That she brought forth her three-volume novel at last;
And she called it "The Ghoul of Mayfair," by "Sirène";
And I read it, re-read it, and read it again.

III.

'Twas about a young girl, whom the gods, in their grace,
Had endowed with a balefully beautiful face;
While her lithe, supple body and limbs were as those
Of a pantheress (*minus* the spots, I suppose).

IV.

And oh! reader, her eyes! and oh! reader, her hair!
They were red, green, blue, lustreless, lava-like. . . . There!
I can't screw my muse to the exquisite pitch
For adjusting exactly the whichness of which!

V.

I may mention at once that she'd dabbled in vice
From her cradle—and found it exceedingly nice:
That she doated on sin—that her only delight
Was in breaking commandments from morning till night.

VI.

And moreover, to deepen her wonderful spell,
She was not only vicious, but artful as well;
For she managed three husbands at once—to begin—
(Just by way of a trifle to keep her hand in).

VII.

The first, a bold indigo-broker was he;
Not young, but as wealthy as wealthy could be—
The next a fond burglar—and last, but not least,
The third was a strapping young Catholic priest!

VIII.

Now, three doating husbands to start with in life
Seems a decent allowance for *any* young wife;
But legitimate trigamy very soon palled
Upon Barbara Blackshepe (for so she was called).

IX.

And it took but a very few pages to tell
How by means of a rope, and a knife, and a well,
And some charcoal, and poison, and powder and shot,
She effectually widowed herself of the lot.

X.

Then she suddenly found that she couldn't control
The yearning for love of her ardent young soul,
So—(this is the cream of the story)—prepare)
She took a large house in the midst of Mayfair:

XI.

Where she started a kind of a sort of a—eh?
Well, a sort of a kind of a—what shall I say?
Like *Turkey*, you know—only just the reverse;
Which, if possible, makes it a little bit worse!

❧

XII.

There were tenors, priests, poets, and parsons—a host!
And Horseguards, and Coldstreams regardless of cost;
While a Leicester-square agent provided a tale
Of select refugees on a liberal scale.

❧

XIII.

The nobility, gentry, and public all round
Her immediate vicinity threatened and frowned:
Some went even so far as to call and complain;
But they never went back to their spouses again!

❧

XIV.

Nay, the very policemen that knocked at the door
To remonstrate were collared, and never seen more;
And 'tis rumoured that *bishops* deserted their lambs
To enrol among "Barbara's Rollicking Rams."

❧

XV.

And their dowdy, respectable, commonplace wives,
And ridiculous daughters all fled for their lives,
And all died with disgusting decorum elsewhere,
To the scorn of "Sirène" and her "Ghoul of Mayfair"!

❧

XVI.

(This light—I might even add *frivolous*—tone
Isn't that of the author, 'tis fair I should own;
Passion hallows each page—guilt ennobles each line;
All this flippant facetiousness, reader, is mine.)

XVII.

To our muttons. Who dances, the piper must pay,
And we can't eat our cake and yet have it, they say;
So we learn with regret that this duck of a pet
Of a dear little widow, she ran into debt.

XVIII.

And the Hebrew came down like the wolf on the fold
(With his waistcoat all gleaming in purple and gold),
And the auctioneer's hammer rang loud in the hall,
And they sold her up—harem and scar'em and all!

XIX.

Then, says she: "There are no more commandments to break:
I have lived—I have loved—I have eaten my cake!"
(Which she had, with a vengeance); so what does she do?
Why, she takes a revolver, and stabs herself through!

❊

XX.

Now, this naughty but nice little Barbara B.
Had, I own, amongst others, demoralised me—
And the tale of her loves had excited me so
That I longed its fair passionate author to know.

XXI.

For, oh! what's more seductive than vice, when you find
It with youth, beauty, genius, and culture combined!
Sweet "Sirène!" How I yearned—how I burned for her! nay,
I went secretly, silently wasting away!

XXII.

Well, at last I beheld her—it did thus befall:
I was wasting away at the Tomkins's ball,
Half inclined to be sick, in my loathing profound
For the mild goody-goody flirtations all round—

XXIII.

When my hostess said suddenly: "*So* glad you came,
Tho' you *may* find us somewhat insipid and tame!
I've a great treat in store for you—turn, and look there!
That's 'Sirène,' who indited '*The Ghoul of Mayfair*.'"

XXIV.

Oh! the wild thrill that shot thro' this passionate heart!
There—before me—alone in her glory—apart
From that milksoppy, maudlin, contemptible throng,
Sat the being I'd yearned for and burned for so long!

XXV.

I respectfully gazed one brief moment—but stop!
For particulars, *vide* design at the top:*
She's that sweet, scornful pet in black velvet you see
Near the nice little man in blue goggles. That's me.

* See picture on preceding page.

Vers Nonsensiques.

Il était un gendarme, à Nanteuil,
Qui n'avait qu'une dent et qu'un œil ;
Mais cet œil solitaire
Était plein de mystère ;
Cette dent, d'importance et d'orgueil.

❧ ❧ ❧ ❧ ❧ ❧ ❧ ❧ ❧

Une vieille (elle était blanchisseuse)
Consultait un docteur à Chevreuse,
Qui, pour calmer ses maux,
Suggéra des bains chauds
D'Elixir de la Grande-Chartreuse.

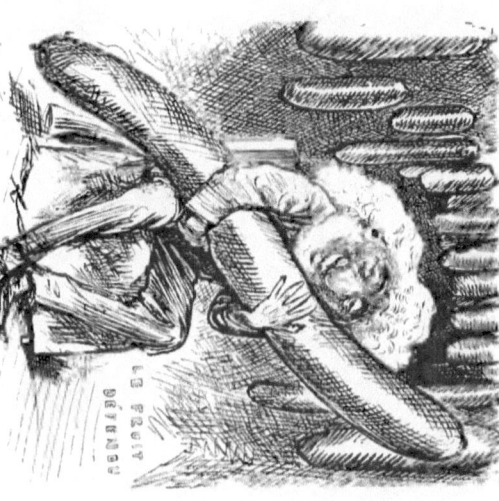

J'ai pour voisin d'en face un vieux Juif
Romanesque, inodore et naïf,
Dont les seules délices
Sont les belles saucisses
Du pays dont Bismarck est natif.

Beau, sans peur, sans reproche, et sans taches,
Chez lui tout—dents, gants, linge, moustaches,
Et lorgnon, sont parfaits;
Mais il perd tous ses frais,
Parcequ'il—laisse tomber ses aches!

Je voudrais être un beau berger blond
Qui jouait du cornet à piston,
Répandit ou sonore
Et doux nom d'Isidore,
Et connût son subjonctif à fond !

À Cologne est un maître d'hôtel
Hors du centre du ventre duquel
Se projette une sorte
De tiroir qui supporte
La moutarde, et le poivre, et le sel.

L'excellent Archevêque de Parme
Soupirait, en versant une larme :
" Que de Liebig l'Extrait
A pour nos dés l'attrait !
Que le Bœuf d'Australie a du charme ! "

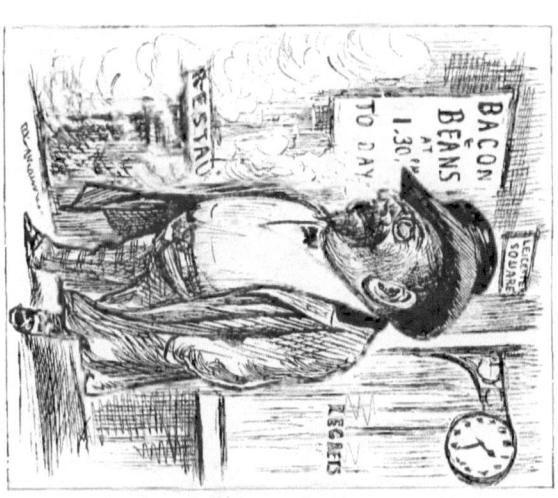

— " O parfum ! idéal de mes rêves ! . . . .
En retins flots jusqu'à moi tu t'élèves !
Oui, j'ai beau t'aspirer,
Je ne puis digérer
Ni ton lard, Pilet Droïn, ni tes fèves ! "

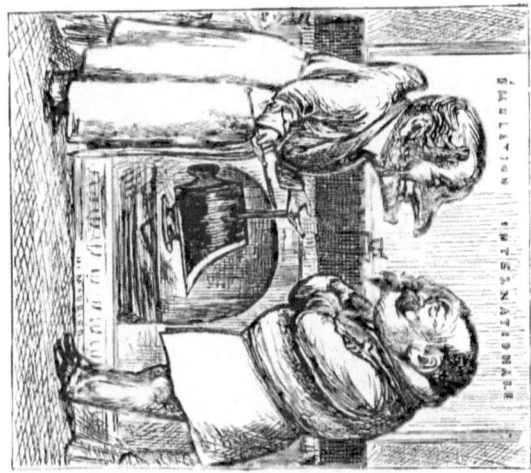

— "Oui, Français, votre patrie est belle,
Et chez vous le soleil étincelle !
Mais l'on n'a pas chez vous
Ces deux objets si doux,
Le Piquant, et la Côte-escoutille !"

Les perpendiculaires rayons
Du soleil illuminaient les fonds
De la mer. Ce chauffage
Fit d'abord fondre au nage
Puis démontisa les poissons.

Un picquum, nommé Picalilli,
Le plus fort des picquaux-Lazuli,
S'éprit d'une picqualli
De chez Crosse et Blacqvelli,
Sut lui plaire, et devint son ami.

Il naquit près de Choisy-le-Roi ;
Le Latin lui causait de l'effroi ;
Et les Mathématiques
Lui donnaient des coliques,
Et le Grec l'enthûmait. Ce fut moi.

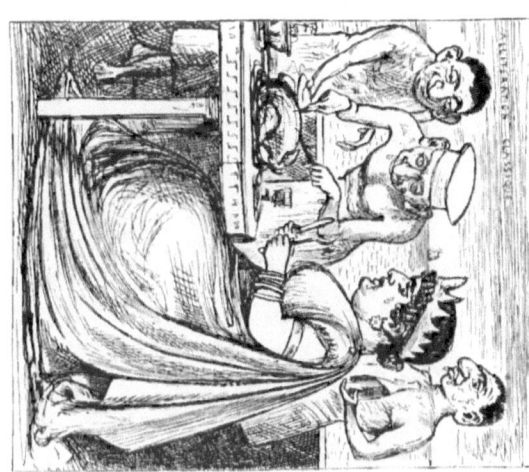

Le chagrin stimulait tant (dit-on)
L'appétit de la chaste Didon,
Qu'à la fuite d'Énée
La belle délaissée
Dîna du dos d'un dodu dindon !

❧ ❧ ❧ ❧ ❧ ❧ ❧ ❧ ❧

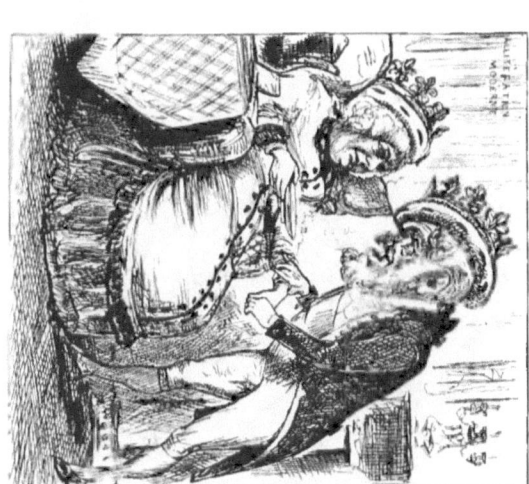

Un vieux duc (le meilleur des époux)
Demandait (en lui tâtant le pouls)
À sa vieille duchesse
(Qu'un vieux catarrhe oppresse) : —
" Et ton thé, t'a-t-il ôté ta toux ? "

Un Marin naufragé (de Doncastre)
Pour prière, au milieu du désastre,
Répétait à genoux
Ces mots simples et doux : —
" Scintillez, scintillez, petit astre ! "

Autrefois, en voyant deux athlètes
Se polichinellier leurs deux têtes,
Monsieur Ponch leur a dit : —
" Rontitontouit !
Quels atouts réguliers vous deux êtes ! "

Un Ténor ambulant (de Bruxelles)
Fasciné par les bières si belles
Qu'on fabrique à Burton,
Entonna la chanson :
" Que je (hic) voudrais avoir vos ailes ! "

À Potsdam, les totaux abstenteurs,
Comme tant d'autres tétotaleurs,
Sont gloutons, omnivores,
Nasoribicolores,
Grands mangeleurs, et terribles duffeurs.

Smith voudrait avoir assez de jeu
Pour parler à cet homme à la roue,
Et pour oser, en cas
Qu'il ne répondit pas,
L'appeler—"Vieux bâton-dans-la-boue!"

Pauvre Édouin ! Angélina t'aimait !
Mais un jour qu'Angélina chantait,
Tu fis une grimace
Qu'elle vit dans la glace. . . . .
Dès ce jour, Pauvre Édouin, c'en est fait !

Il était un Hébreu de Hambourg,
Qui creva d'un mauvais calembourg,
Qu'il eut l'audace extrême
De commettre en carême,
Un Dimanche, au milieu d'Edinbourg.

⇒C ⇒C ⇒C ⇒C ⇒C ⇒C ⇒C ⇒C

Cinq fois veuf, il a cinq belle-mères,
Dont il fait les délices si chères
Qu'elles vivent chez lui
Pour charmer son ennui . . . .
Ses regrets n'en sont pas moins sincères.

Je me suis demandé bien souvent
Ce que c'est qu'un " Breton Bretonnant " ?
N'en déplaise à personne,
Quand un Breton " bretonne, "
Par où " bretonne "-t-il ? . . . Et comment ?

Chaque époque a ses grands noms sonores ;
Or, de tous ces défunts cocholores,
Le moral Faudon,
Michel Ange, et Johnson
(Le Docteur), sont les plus awfuls bores !

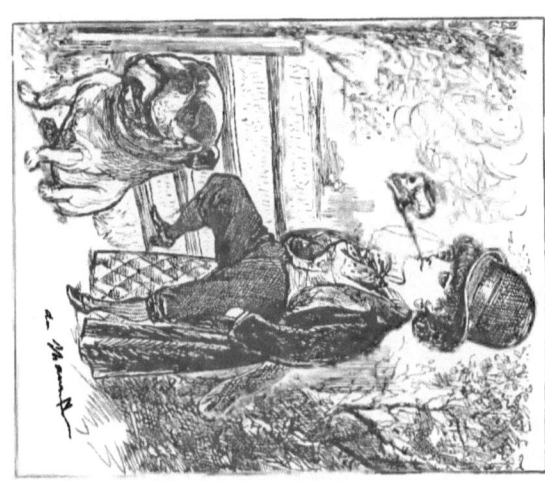

Il existe une Espinsière à Tours,
Un peu vite, et qui porte toujours
Un nisteur peau-de-phoque,
Un chapeau bilicoque,
Et des nicrobocqueurs en velours.

❧ ❧ ❧ ❧ ❧ ❧ ❧ ❧ ❧

" Qu'un rôti de gigot, ma Lucie,
À trois heures soit prêt, je te prie :
Qu'il soit tendre, fumant,
Et d'un jus abondant,
Et quel meilleur plat-il-u-can there be ? "

Un Spondée, envieux d'un Dactyle,
Son voisin dans un vers de Virgile,
Blaguait à tout propos
Ses trois pieds inégaux,
L'assignait, et lui chauffait la bile.

❧ ❧ ❧ ❧ ❧ ❧ ❧ ❧ ❧ ❧

Il était un brignol de la Drouille,
Dont l'esbrocq turlupait la frambouille,
Et qui raccolbochait
Son splénif, et borgliait
En Binclons: "Rampognons !... je dégrouille !!"

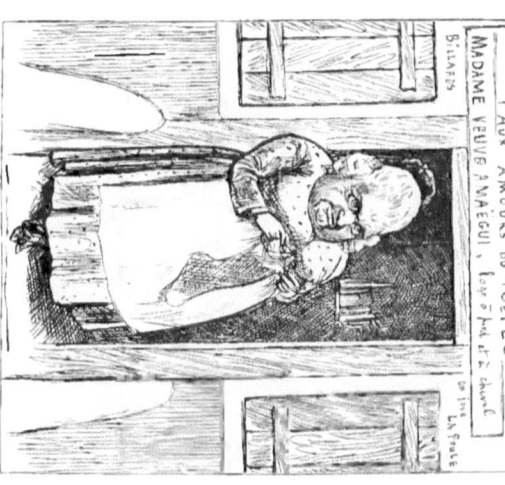

L'Andalouse (*Marquise et Lionne*),
Qui naguère habitait Barcelone,
Et démoralisait
Tout le Sieur de Musset,
Vient d'ouvrir une auberge à Bayonne.

"O jument de la nuit, ombre sombre !
D'où viens-tu ?—de ces radis sans nombre ?—
— Ou viens-tu cette fois
De ce lapin gallois ?—
Ou viens-tu—de ce maudit concombre ?"

"Cassez-vous, cassez-vous, cassez-vous,
O mer, sur vos froids gris cailloux !"
    Ainsi traduisait Laure
    Au profit d'Isidore
(Bon jeune homme, et son futur époux).

" I am *joli*, I am poet. I dwell
Rupert Street, at the fifth. I am swell.
    And I sing tralala,
    And I love my mamma,
And the English, I speaks him quite well !"

L'Onglays à Parry.

UNG mattaing j'etty dong Paree,
Ay tristey je regardy
Le purple kee se promenay
Le long dew Bullyvardy.

Je funy ay je ravy, may
Partoo l'onwee se trouvy;
Avec une petty tube de pyle
De tongs ong tong, je buvy.

Assee devong le caffy, donc,
Je buvy ay je fumy,
Ay j'admiray le joly mond,
Les elegoug costumy.

Tongtó c'etait ung deputay
Lisong le *Charryvarry*;
Tongtote une dam de kalitay
Kee sortay song song marry.

Epwee day fam de tute espayce
Ong tray grand variety—
Des actreece, ay day fam dew mond,
Day bonn, ay day grisetty:

• •

Epwee Messiew les Etudiong,
Tray sal, ay tray mal painyay,
Ay kee sortay de n'amport oo,
(Excepty de se bainyay).

Tongtote oon belle voiture, epwee
Une villang viel fiark, ay
Ung Mossoo, faisong sauty song
Cheval, poor ayt remarkay.

Epwee, partoo des militairs!
O tempora! O mory! ....
Kelks etty view, kelks etty june,
May tutes etay decory.

Kelks etty june, kelks etty viell,
Ay kelks, nee l'ung nee l'oty;
May tutes avvy l'air con-
tong d'ellmayn—
Ay le reste avvy tute la beautay.

Ongfang le Pranks

Ampayrial,
Song pair, ay tute sà sweeter,
Assee sewer une long petty cheval
Kée n'ally par trô veeter.

K'ong sudang, s'offrit à may ziew
Croisong de l'oter coty,
Ung pair, une mair, une belle june feel,
De may compatrioy.

Là mair avay day blongs cheevew,
Là pheel, day cheevew dory;
Le pair n'ong avvy pardertoo,
Ay parissay se bory.

Le pair portay song pairaplwee,
Là mair say jewpongs porty:
Là pheel ne porty reangdertoo,
Elle avait ung escorty.

Car, plang d'amoor, a côty d'elle
Etait ung tray distangy . . .
O, hang it! what's the French for "swell?"
And what's the rhyme for "angy?"

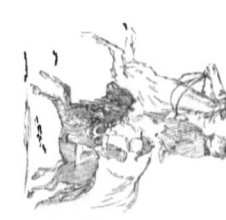

Elle sombly bowkoo aymay lwee;
Il parissay s'adory!
*O fortunatos nimium
Si sua bona nôr(int!)*

Hay biang, cette coople amoroo,
Ke tute le mond regardy,
Etay plew bel ke tute le mond
Sewer tute la Bullyardy.

Ay cette viell mair, ay cet view pair
Etay plew respectarble
Ke presker tute les abatongs
De cette grond veal dew diarble.

Alors, je pongsay a là pheel
(Ay bowkoo je regretty)
Ke j'avvy laissy dairyar mwaw
(Portong le nong de Bety).

Au souvenir de ma sheree,
May pulsationg se haty;
L'annoor saccray de là patree
Causay mong cure de batty.

Appelay veeter le garsong,
Ay dear: "Combiang çà couty?"
Ay donny der soo poor lweenaym
C'est l'affaire d'une minuty.

Payay là note exorbiong
À l'honnue oo je demuray—
Pronder le Shmang-de-fair-dew-Nord—
C'est l'affaire d'ung card'ury.

Aprays oon tray grossiay passarge
Ay tute malard ke j'etty,
Je coury met mong pover cure
Aux pover piay de Betty.

"Oh vullyvoosayter mong chair fam?
Oh vullyvoosayt? repondy!"....
Ay sà reponse affirmateeve,
C'est l'affaire d'une secondy!

Car Betty, c'etty une see bonne pheel!
Là meillewer pheel dew monder!
Ay Betty, c'etty là plew belle pham
De Bloomsbury, à Londer!

Ne soydoncpar bowkoo sewerprees,
See voo voyay parayter
2 jollypettygarsongs dew main àrge
Dongs t perambulator.

TWO THRONES.

OH, Beauty, peerless as thou art,
    And wide thy range, and keen thy dart,
    And meek the captives of thy bow,
    Inconstant beats the manly heart—
        The present Bard's extremely so!

Wit, Wisdom, Strength, and Valour meet
    (The Bard amongst them), at thy feet
    To kneel in homage, as of old;
    Yet turn a rival Queen to greet,
        Whose crown is of a purer gold!

Preen as thou wilt thy feathers fine,
    A gift is hers, by grace divine,
    Even more potent to enthral,
    O Bird of Paradise, than thine,
        The hearts and souls of one and all!

And what avail thy gilded crest,
    The silver shimmer of thy breast,
    The glories of thy painted wing,
    If, yielding to the Bard's behest,
        The Nightingale vouchsafe to sing!

A LOVE-AGONY.

❧ O an thou be, that faintest in such wise,
With love-wan eyelids on love-wanton eyes,
Fain of thyself! I faint, adoring thee,
Fain of thy kisses, fainer of thy sighs,
Yet fainest, love! an thou wert fain of me,
So an thou be!

❧ Yea, lo! for veriest fainness faint I, Sweet,
Of thy spare bosom, where no shadows meet,
And small strait hip, and weak delicious knee!
For joy thereof I swoon, and my pulse-beat
Is as of one that wasteth amorously,
So an thou be!

❧ Shepherd art thou, or nymph, that ailest there?
Lily of Love, or Rose? Search they, who care,
Thy likeness for a sign! For, verily,
Naught reck I, Fairest, so an thou be but Fair!
E'en as he recks not, that hath limnèd thee,
So an thou Be!

"With her soft eyelids on her wearied eyes."

A Simple Story.

I.

THERE lived a youth (he liveth yet),
   And Richard was he christened;
And well he played the flageolet,
   And all the ladies listened;
And some were even heard to say
   His brow was handsome (in its way).

II.

But Richard met Ben Ball, a man
   All chest, and cheek, and shoulder,
And ever so much bigger than
   Himself, though little older:
Whose biceps Richard felt and found
It measured fifteen inches round!

III.

Now this demoralised him quite;
   And then he took to reading
The naughty books that ladies write
   And found there, with exceeding
Dismay, that ladies' heroes are
Wild, wicked men, and muscular!

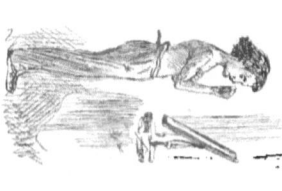

IV.

Then in high dudgeon did he use
   To feel himself all over;
But little sinew, and no thews
   Could Richard's thumbs discover:
And wickedness is rarely met
In men that play the flageolet.

V.

But 'twas not yet too late to mend;
He got dumb-bells, and shyly
He took the counsel of a friend
    ("*Experimentum vili*")
And tried them first on his left arm,
And found they acted like a charm!

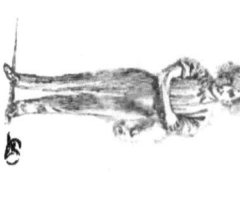

VI.

Much bigger waxed his biceps, but
    When this left arm was finished,
The left lobe of his occiput
    Had sensibly diminished;
So then he went it, right and all,
To make his nut symmetrical!

VII.

His nut soon got so hardened that
    It hurt you when you hit it;
Nor could his hatter find a hat
    (Already made) to fit it,
So marvellously small it grew,
As all may judge from this back view.

VIII.

At length a happy day came round
    (Which *I* was there, and drew it)
When Richard lifted from the ground
    A paving-stone, and threw it
Almost one foot three-quarters high!
And that with ladies standing by!!

IX.

Not only that ; he, on his head
　So dexterously caught it,
That all the ladies present said
　They never should have thought it !
And even I could not but own
　'Twas hard lines for the paving-stone !

X.

Next day he caught a cold, alack !
　And all his muscles vanished,
But none of his old brains came back
　Which his dumb-bells had banished ;
And not a rack was left behind
　Of what he chose to call his mind !

XI.

Poor Richard now (O have you met
　Him lately) has grown bitter ;
For, when he plays the flageolet
　The ladies talk and titter ;
And no one ever thinks his brow
　In any way good-looking now !

XII.

O little men, who wish to please,
　Be wiser than poor Dick ! shun
Big friends with brawny biceps,
　And female works of fiction ;
But stick to music all your might,
　Or be cut out. And serve you right !

A Ballad of Blunders.

(AFTER SWINBURNE'S BALLAD OF BURDENS.)

THE Blunder of Short Garments. Thou shalt wear

Thy supple thighs in sheaths of splendid fit,
Much use whereof shall surely render bare
The mystery, yea, the very threads of it;
And cold shall seize thee standing; should'st thou sit,
Thy skin shall vex thee with its tenderness;
Or stoop, thy perilous underseam shall split;
This is the end of every man's excess.

The Blunder of Gay Seasons. Strange delight;
Thy seething garb shall cleave to thee, and cling;
Thy red wet palm shall reek beneath the white;
And fierce black shining leather bite and sting,
A future of sore troubles gathering;
The dawn shall send thee, cold and comfortless,
Creeping along the kerb, an abject thing.
This is the end of every man's excess.

The Blunder of Much Music. Sit thee down,
Nay, stop thine ears, and sleep. For verily,
She that is playing heedeth not thy frown,
And she that singeth takes no thought for thee;
And song shall follow song till thou shalt be
Smitten and bitten with fierce restlessness
To bite and smite in turn, or turn to flee;
This is the end of every man's excess.

The Blunder of Great Banquets. Out of sight,
Beyond the reach of hands that heal for gain,
The dish of thy desire and thy delight
Shall vex thy sleep. Thou shalt behold again
The Lord Knight Mayor, thy host, as King of Pain;
And lo, the worthy Lady Mayoress
As Queen of Pleasure in thy fond heart shall reign;
This is the end of every man's excess.

The Blunder of Long Speeches. Thou shalt burn
To see men whisper, and thy voice grow thick,
And shame shall stain thee red and white by turn,
And all thy wine shall rise and make thee sick;
And short swift sobs shall take thy breath betw-hic!
And in thy skull shall be much emptiness,
And in thy stead, the likeness of a stick.
This is the end of every man's excess.

The Blunder of Late Hours. Leave thy sad bed;
See what strange things shall grieve thy straining sight:
Stray broken glass to greet the dawn; grey dead
Strewn ashes of the weeds of thy delight;
Sick sterile leavings of the hot fierce night;
Yet must thou bend thee to thy business
Thy brain to brood; thy tremulous hand to write;
This is the end of every man's excess.

The Blunder of Strong Spirits; warm and sweet,
   Or cold without, and pale; whereof to tread
The wild wet ways is perilous to thy feet,
   And in thine eyes, where green was, lo, the red;
And where thy sinew, soft weak fat instead;
   Burning of heart, and much uneasiness
About thy girdle, and aching in thine head;
   This is the end of every man's excess.

The Blunder of Much Rhyming. If thou write
   That once again that should be once for all,
These market-men will buy thy black and white
   Till thy keen swift full fervent ways shall fall
On sated ears; thy stinging sweetness pall;
   And barren memories of thy bright success
Shall burst in thee the bladder of thy gall;
   This is the end of every man's excess.

The Blunder of Long Ballads. Bide in peace;
   For when the night is near, the day shall die,
And when the day shall dawn the night shall cease,
   And all things have an end of all; and I
An end of this, for that my lips are dry,
   And the eleventh hour's exceeding heaviness
Doth overweigh mine eyelid on mine eye . . . .
   This is the end of every man's excess.

MORAL.

Poets, who tread the fast and flowerful way,
   Heed well the burden these sad rhymes impress;
Pleasure is first, and then the time to pay;
   This is the end of every man's excess.

CHATOUILLARD.

The Rise and Fall of the Jack Spratts.

A Tale of Modern Art and Fashion.

Part 1.

N a beautiful old suburb of London, undesecrated, as yet, by steam or telegraph-wires, and surrounded by low-lying flowery meads, through which the Thames would still meander occasionally, as it had been wont to do in days long gone by, dwelt Jack Spratt, a handsome, genial, and simple-minded young painter. He had a girl-wife of lofty stature, and truly transcending loveliness, a gift of which she seemed as yet unconscious.

They were unknown to fame, and not of exalted birth; but they had refined tastes, pretty manners, and affectionate dispositions, and were unto each other even as the apple of the eye. Their united ages amounted to thirty-nine brief summers. They had twins (a boy and a girl), as beautiful as the day, whom they loved with an exceeding love, and who loved them back again with all the singleness of their two little child hearts, that beat as one. "Oh, really *quite* too fortunate! . . had they but known" (as Virgil would no doubt have exclaimed, had he but been an Englishman, and lived to make the acquaintance of Mr. and Mrs. J. Spratt)!

Their house was of red brick, smothered in ivy, and had been built about Queen Anne's time, or before, and never repaired since, nor meddled with in any way whatever. It stood by itself in a small old-fashioned garden, surrounded by once peach-laden walls that crumbled to the touch, and overrun with nettles, thistles, marigolds, sunflowers, and poppies; a trellised arbour of sweet pea half buried a sun-dial in its fragrant gloom; and there was a nice little green pond. Apple-trees and pear-trees, leafless and long past fruit bearing, but beautifully gnarled, grew rank as in an orchard, and on to a luxuriant lawn that had never known the scythe, opened the pretty studio, which was full of blue china, round mirrors, faded tapestry, carved oak-chests, high-backed chairs, brazen sconces, mediæval arms and armour, an organ with beautifully painted pipes but no bellows, and other musical instruments, such as sackbuts and psalteries, a harpsichord without any strings, and a dulcimer that had been turned into an eight-day clock, but could never be got to go. The dust lay thick on all these pretty things, and toned them into harmony. Studio, house, and garden were pervaded with a subtle fragrance, significant of old associations, which arose in the soft summer twilight from time-honoured, ruined, and all but forgotten drains.

Jack Spratt also gloried in the possession of two beautiful and costly lay figures, representing a mother and a child, the only modern objects in the house, whose open countenances and curiously-wrought limbs, duly draped, he would never tire of painting, while his lovely wife sat by, darning his socks, may be, or embroidering some quaint device, as she read to him aloud old tales of chivalry, to which he was extremely partial, while the twins frolicked at her pretty feet. This work done, after a frugal meal of bread and honey in the parlour, they would hie them to the flowery mead; and there, in the golden sunset, she would ply her spinning-wheel, and softly sing some ancient ballad in a foreign tongue, while the twins gambolled in lamb-like innocence around.

They made a pretty picture, these happy children and their beautiful young mother, and the trees, and the grass, and the winding river, bathed in the glories of eventide; and in the midst of it all, Jack Spratt would be inspired to close his eyes, and reverently,

"The Spratts at home."

regretfully, recall to mind the grand old sunsets, by the grand Old Masters, in the National Gallery, and the quaint old children and mothers by Bogofogo, Antima Cassaro, Vecchio Coccoloro, Fra Stoggiato di Vernicelli, Sarsaparillo dello Strando, and other painters of that ante-pra-Raphaelite school; and, in the depths of his bliss, a feeling of discouragement would steal over him as he thought of those immortal works, showing thereby that he was a true artist, ever striving after the light. He little dreamt in his modesty, that, young and inexperienced though he might be, his pictures were even quainter than theirs; for not only could he already draw, colour, compose, and put into perspective quite as badly as they did, but he had over them the advantage of a real lay figure to copy, whereas they had to content themselves with the living model.

The amusements of this happy pair were of the simplest, healthiest, and most delightful kind; they never went to the play, nor to balls or dances, which they thought immodest—(indeed they were not even asked)—nor read such things as novels, magazines, or the newspaper; nor visited exhibitions of modern art, which they held in contempt, as they did all things modern; but they skipped, with single and double rope, and played battledore and shuttlecock, and hunt the slipper, and puss in the corner, and hide-and-seek, and such like little innocent old games; and they were devoted to music, not that of the present day, which they despised, nor that of the future, of which they had never heard; nor English music, which was not old enough; but music of the early continental school, with nice easy tunes, which they could learn to sing in unison, and early French and Italian words, which appealed to their fond hearts with all the hidden power of a language they loved but did not understand. Their voices were musical and low. They sang even the liveliest ditties to a slow sad measure of their own, and in the sweet but homely accent of their native London. The reader can hardly realize the effects that early French or Italian strains of a festive nature, with festive words to match, can produce on a musical Frenchman or Italian of the present day, when rendered in this unsophisticated manner by such performers as Mr. and Mrs. Jack Spratt.

They were not without friends, carefully chosen on the combined principles of natural and Holbsonian selection. They were few, but true and trusty, with remarkably fine heads for a painter; their gait, gestures, grammar, and personal habits were mediæval; their deportment grave, sad, and very strange; for the death of the early Italian Masters still weighed on their souls with all the force of some recent domestic bereavement, and they always behaved with the solemnity that befitted them as chief mourners, speaking of the dead in hushed and reverential whispers; not that they conversed very freely or very often; they were much given to long periods of thoughtful silence, which were held sacred by each other, and only broken now and then by flashes of a sad strange merriment, that would have puzzled an outsider immensely. But, buoyed up as they were by brave hopes of the past and a firm faith in better days gone by, they were not unhappy. They looked on themselves, and each other, and the Jack Spratts, and were looked upon by the Jack Spratts in return, as the sole incarnation on this degenerate earth of all such good as had still managed to survive there; and so they were always telling each other, and every one else they met. And no wonder, for they were marvellously accomplished; being each of them painter, sculptor, architect, poet, critic, and engraver, all in one; and all this without ever having learnt, but through a mere effort of the will, and by mutual consent, as it were; and if you were to mention to them the name of any world-renowned follower of any of those arts in the present day, they would coldly reply:— "We don't know any painters!" or, "We don't know any poets!" as the case might be, and walk off in an opposite direction; and after that you would find it very difficult to continue the conversation.

As for the Royal Academy, they held it in merely passive contempt, and were satisfied with never having heard the names of its most celebrated members. Their especial scorn was reserved for that

school of Art which finds its home on the walls of the Grosvenor Gallery; they regarded its disciples as renegades, and its gifted leader as a base apostate, who, having once known the better way, had chosen to depart from it, and had been branded in consequence with the indelible Hall Mark of ineffaceable popular renown. In extenuation of such extreme views, it must be admitted that the authorities of the Grosvenor Gallery had not invited Jack Spratt and his trusty friends to exhibit there; not through any ill-will, but because they had never heard of them.

Their appearance in the streets of busy London was in no way remarkable, for they walked abroad in shapeless hats, long cloaks, and cheap garments of an ordinary reach-me-down description; but often, when they met at the Jack Spratts' in the gloaming, or at evensong, or Curfew time, as they would alternately call it, they would doff their ponchos, slip their ready-made trousers, and display themselves, regardless of expense, in the outward bravery of that early Italian time they held so dear; and all this without ever departing from the grave and impressive demeanour that was habitual to them.

Sorrow and sickness seldom visit those who lead such pure, simple, and innocent lives. In their hours of sorrow, the Spratts and their friends would find comfort in gazing at some pretty combination of form and colour; such as a dead frog lying on a blue china plate in the sun, or a cracked sackbut with a peacock's feather sticking out of its bung-hole. Their only abiding grief was a hideous red pillar-post which stood outside the gates of their pretty dwelling; and so much did they loath this undecorative object, that they never used it, on principle, but even in bad weather would walk half a mile to post such few letters as they ever had occasion to write. Indeed, most of these had been written to the Vestry, demanding that the pillar-post should be removed, on the score of its unsightliness, and offering to replace it by a new sun-dial, designed, free of charge, by Jack Spratt, from the old one in his arbour, on condition that the parish should bear the expense of the original material, its carving according to Jack Spratt's design, and its subsequent erection. But the Vestry had taken no notice of these appeals.

In their hours of sickness alone the Spratts were as other people, and sent immediately for the nearest medical practitioner (or leech, as they preferred to call him); their only sickness to speak of had arisen from once feasting medievally on an old roast peacock, in company with the trusty friends, who had also been taken very bad on that occasion; and they ever afterwards avoided that dish, but at their banquets would have the peacock's head and what was left of its tail tacked on to some more digestible bird, which, duly roasted beforehand, and allowed to cool, would thus adorn their board with borrowed plumes before it was carved and eaten, and so please their aesthetic sense without making them sick afterwards; a very wise precaution; for they were very much given to such old-fashioned hospitality, these Spratts: although their acquaintance was by their own choice (so they said) rather limited; for as staunch Radicals, they hated the aristocracy, whose very existence they ignored; shunned the professional class, which they scorned, on account of its scientific and utilitarian tendency; and loathed the middle class, from which they had sprung, because it was Philistine; and although they professed to deeply honour the working man, they very wisely managed to see as little of him as they possibly could; and thus, living for each other, and their chosen friends, they haughtily held aloof from the outer world, which, it must be owned, betrayed no wish whatever to lure them from their seclusion.

Although the kind of felicity we have tried to depict may not commend itself to the taste of the general reader, he cannot fail to see that for such unworldly people as the Spratts, it leaves nothing to be desired. Youth, health, simplicity of life, a modest competency, self-respect, friendship, domestic affection, the love of Art, innocence of mundane ambition, blameless aspirations and regrets, everything seems combined to make their existence happy and blessed; not to mention that belief in themselves and each other and all that belongs

to them, which Mr. Punch looks upon as the highest conducement (if he may forge a word) to earthly bliss. He has dwelt at length, and with a lingering fondness, on this idyllic picture of the Spratts' home, and the gentle life they led there. Grave it in your mind, good reader, for there are few such homes in England; nay, that you may grave it in your mind the better, Mr. Punch has subtilely limned for you a cartoon showing the Spratts at home, in their pretty garden, with the twins and the trusty friends, all mediævally arrayed, around them. Jack Spratt and his wife are playing "cat's cradle," the twins are revolving quaint conceits in their æsthetic little minds; the friends are fondly lute-playing, or poring over old myths, and musing sadly on the light of other days; what time Sally the Cook is dishing up a cold roast capon (which, in her haste, she has unfortunately peacocked the wrong way), and her distant policeman looks over the wall, with one eye for her, and one for the cold roast capon. Say, reader, is not it a fair, glad, gracious picture?

Part 2.

T happened one day that Jack Spratt's beautiful lay figure had to go back to its maker's, in order to be cleaned, mended, and restuffed; and the happy thought occurred to Jack Spratt that he might as well take a respite from serious Art-work and paint a portrait of his wife, as she sat there darning one of his socks and reading aloud from a black-letter edition of *Jack and the Bean Stalk*, whose adventures never seemed to pall on the Spratts and their friends.

Now Mrs. Spratt's form and features had not been cast in an early Italian mould; her maiden name was Maloney, and her papa had kept a leading oil and Italian warehouse in Finsbury; which was, indeed, the only Italian feature in the family. Her mother had been a lovely Lancashire lass; and Mrs. Spratt had raven hair, violet eyes, ruby lips, an ivory brow, and a skin made of the whitest lily and the reddest rose. Her little head was poised on a long thick creamy neck, while her tall supple figure erred if at all on the side of a too super-abundant exuberance; but her waist was very small, and so were her proudly arched feet; and her dimpled little white hands had not been made for sock-darning, or any such house drudgery; but to be tightly-gloved in all that Paris can furnish of the best in perfumed kid, five and three-quarters, *gris perle*.

It is, perhaps, too much to say that Jack Spratt did the same justice to all these charms as he had always done to those of his lay figure; but he produced something so different from anything he had ever produced before, that the trusty friends, who were scandalised beyond measure, repeatedly exclaimed that if *that* were Art, then the Old Masters must be *wrong*!

Jack Spratt, however, in spite of the trusty friends, had it framed, called it *Ye Playre Sockque-darrnêre*, and forwarded it to the Royal Academy, much as he had persistently scorned that institution; and the Royal Academicians, who had persistently rejected, year after year, the pictures Jack Spratt and his friends had as persistently sent there, accepted this one; and owing, perhaps, to a little difference among themselves about one of their own works, hung it on the line, in a place of honour in the large room, No. 3, where it made such a sensation that a plucky Baronet bought it at the private view.

Thus Jack woke up one morning, and found himself famous.

Of the Art critics, some proclaimed in him the advent of the long-yearned-for nineteenth-century genius, whose holy mission it was to redeem the Art of our day from the loathsome degradation into which it had fallen; and with the generous intolerance of youth, branded as snobs and ruffians those who could not quite agree with them; others, with the calm benignity of age, pronounced both Jack and his admirers to be perfectly harmless, but incurably imbecile; so that old friends quarrelled, and united families fell out, and all the world was set by the ears through Jack Spratt's little sock-darner; dealers came down on his studio like the wolf on the fold; and so great was the crowd round this picture, that the Royal Academy stationed a couple of mounted Policemen near it, a thing which had never been done in Burlington House before; and many a shilling they brought to the Royal Academy—those two mounted Policemen; and a very happy thought it was to have them there!

The upshot of all this was, that the plucky Baronet, who had purchased the little sock-darner, called at Jack's studio with his

The News of the ...

Lady, and they were much charmed with all they saw. This Baronet could not only tell a pretty picture when he saw one, but also a pretty face when he saw one. Most Baronets are equal to that; and as for my Lady, a good-natured and impulsive person, she was quite beside herself with delight at the notion of Genius painting Beauty, while Beauty darned the socks of Genius. She immediately looked upon Mr. and Mrs. Jack Spratt as a pet little invention of her own; and before she had been five minutes in their company, invited them to a "small and early" at her mansion, in Belgrave Square. By this time also the Spratts' life-long prejudice against the aristocracy had quite evaporated; and they accepted this invitation with alacrity.

Well, the Spratts duly attended that "small and early," attired in their very best. Mr. Punch forgets what Mrs. Spratt's very best consisted of at this particular period of her career; but rather thinks it must have been a broidered wimple, surcinctured with a golden jirripipe over a welted chatsel-smock of watchet sergedusoy, lined with shalloon, and edged with vair, or possibly ermine.

Jack Spratt so far gave way to the conventionalities of modern life as to wear a gent's evening suit complete for three-seventeen-six (made to order by a suburban tailor for this special occasion), and put a smart peacock's feather in his button-hole. At the same time, in order to show how simple and unworldly he really was, he sported a watch-guard made of common pack-thread, and left his luxuriant locks untouched by the comb.

They got to the "small and early" an hour and a half too soon, and had to disport themselves alone in those gilded Belgravian Saloons until the company had done dinner. Presently the great and gay came trooping in, and the Spratts mingled with the glittering throng, and liked it very much, especially Mrs. S., who thought it very civil and attentive; it is not too much to say that she attracted far more notice than any of the highborn ladies there, even the Papuan ambassadress.

In the course of the evening, Mrs. Spratt was prevailed upon by

64

her amiable hostess (whom nobody had ever been known to resist) to sit on a stool, as she had done in the famous picture, and darn a beautiful blue and yellow silk sock of the Baronet's to a running accompaniment on the pianoforte by one of our rising composers, who had been cunningly invited on purpose, while Spratt was made to stand by in the attitude of an early Italian Master consumed by a pure but wasting passion.

This impromptu tableau had an immense success, and our simple friends were the lions of the evening, and passed a delightful time, and quickly, but firmly, resolved that this outer world they had taken such pains to shun had its charms, and that they would certainly cease to shun it in future.

Mrs. Spratt's deep-rooted dislike to the female dress of the present day did not last much longer than her life-long prejudice against the aristocracy. The very next morning after that small and early, she discarded the medieval garments she had hitherto worn with such disdain for the eccentricities of modern fashion, and put herself into the hands of the best dress-maker in town. She had always looked lovely in her quaint old-fashioned attire, although the irreverent outside world had been wont to smile thereat as she took her walks abroad; but oh! how far lovelier she looked in the latest Paris mode, with chamois-leather underclothing, and tightly clinging skirts that showed her as she really was! The simple-minded Jack hardly recognised her, and in the depths of this modest mind he made comparisons between his wife and his boy figure, that were not always to the advantage of the latter.

He also bespoke the services of a fashionable West-end Artist; no more suburban evening suits for him! but a beautiful dress-coat, with black velvet collar, and watered-silk facings; a white waist-coat, with three coral buttons to match the shirt-studs, only bigger; trousers cut rather wide; neat pumps, and black silk socks, with white clocks; and for his button-hole a *Stephanotis*, in a little glass tube full of water to keep it fresh.

One invitation leads to another, when the invited are as beautiful as Mrs. Spratt, and as clever and modest as her husband, and especially when they possess such unhackneyed social accomplishments; soon she could scarcely see her lovely face in the Chippendale mirror over the front parlour mantelpiece, for the coroneted notes and cards of invitation she was able to stick there.

It is true that the plucky Baronet's Lady had dropped the Spratts a week after she had taken them up (in favour of a female Æolian harpist, with a blind Albino brother, and a very clever and faithful dog), but during that week she had raved about them so much, and presented them to so many people, that they were fairly launched on the sea of London Society, and no longer thought much of Baronets and their good ladies.

As in duty bound, Mrs. Spratt was presented at Court. She also purchased a *Peerage*, &c., and learnt therein who was connected with whom, and all about everybody worth knowing; and grew to talk in sympathetic tones about the dear Marchioness, and poor Lady Anna Maria, who was such a martyr to rheumatism; and such like smart people; and you couldn't mention any Lady of decent fashion before her but what she would ask, "Who *was* she, by the bye?" if she didn't know; or if she did, she would insist on telling you, whether you wanted or not.

Not the least important result of these genealogical studies was that she established to her own satisfaction that the John Spratts must be descended from the same stock as the St. John d'Esperats, of Chalkstoneshire, and were consequently entitled to bear the same crest, which she forthwith had engraved on her notepaper and envelopes; and on suddenly discovering that the head and last remaining scion of that ancient but impecunious house had recently cut his throat in a fit of *delirium tremens*, after having been publicly kicked out of the Kingston race-course for welching, she felt the family disgrace so keenly that it quite upset her; and although she made Jack Spratt wear a hat-band, and went into slight mourning herself, just for decency's sake, she would not allow the sad event to be mentioned or discussed in her presence.

As for Jack, he was in the seventh heaven at all this, as well indeed he might be; not that he thought his wife's beauty had anything to do with their sudden rise in the social scale; although modest to a fault, he felt that Society was only honouring itself in honouring such genius as his, but it pleased and touched him to see how cordially, for his sake, Society had also welcomed the one he loved best, and his bosom swelled with manly pride, to see how well she bore herself and held her own.

How often it happens that the great male Spratts of this world do not achieve fame, and thus become ornaments of Society, and worth its notice, till their females have tarnished their bright scales and hardened their pretty fins in household cares, and the nursing of innumerable Spratlings (or shall we call them whitebait). So that sometimes, the great ones of the earth, and especially the would-be great ones, and more especially their womankind, and most especially such of their womankind as are neither useful nor ornamental, would gladly welcome the gifted husband, and leave the thrifty wife out in the cold; and gifted husbands are sometimes so supple-backed, and thrifty wives so meek and lowly, as to acquiesce in such an arrangement. **In** which case, Mr. Punch, who really loves the poor in spirit, and can thoroughly appreciate grovelling self-abasement in others (if it be only genuine and sincere), hardly knows which to commend the most, the husband or the wife.

Nor is he at all unsympathetic, when he sees some titled lady-radical, who rates modest (male) worth higher than Norman blood; or better still, some fourth-rate woman of fashion, say some rich contractor's wife, or some wealthy stock-broker's lion-hunting widow, who wishes to make her house attractive; pressing her hospitality on some small new rickety lion, with a sprouting mane, say an amateur tenor, while she altogether forgets to invite his maneless but

faithful consort, who can only roar at home; and if said lion, such as he is, accepts said invitation, and allows his lioness to be passed over and ignored, even by the greatest lady in the land, it suits Mr. Punch's humour to get himself introduced to that lion, and after the usual compliments to hiss into his ear,

"Doff thy lion's hide,
And hang a livery on those recreant limbs."

And he must be uncommon smart at repartee for an amateur tenor if he can parry such a home-thrust as that.

Mais, revenons à nos ——. By the bye, what is the French for Spratts? Perhaps there are no such fish or people in that democratic country, so we will return instead to the trusty friends, who, thank Heaven! are to be found in all countries. In this country, alas! which is not democratic, trusty friends who are not asked to dine and dance with the Aristocracy, very seldom tolerate those who are. They say spiteful things calculated to take one down; and Mrs. Spratt did not like to be taken down. It was especially distasteful to her when she happened quite by accident to mention the dear Marchioness, and poor Lady Anna Maria with her rheumatics, or to bewail Lord George's unhappy *mésalliance* with an attorney's daughter, that these tried and trusty friends should yawn, or hum, or whistle out of tune, as they would invariably do on such occasions; moreover, their innocent prattle about the grand Old Masters (peace to whose ashes !) had begun very much to pall on Mrs. Spratt; and she had grown to dislike the cut of the trusty friends' clothes, and the way they wore their hair, and other mediæval ways they had, so that a coolness gradually made itself felt between them. At last they fell out altogether, sad to say, and parted. It happened thus :—

Jack Spratt and his wife had been driven on a drag to Hurlingham by a noble lord of their acquaintance. Mrs. Spratt had sat on the box-seat, and with the exception of the two grooms (and of her husband, who had been put inside), there had sat nobody behind her back of humbler rank than the younger son of an Earl. After a delightful afternoon, they were set down at their own door. There was to have been a dress evening with the trusty friends at Jack's house that night; and one of them, Peter Leonardo Pye, was to have read a series of original poems, entitled *Dank Kisses from Mildewed Lips*. Mrs. Spratt bade a regretful farewell to all the smart young men, and on entering her dwelling with a sigh, she found the trusty friends assembled in the hall. They were austerely pulling off their trousers, and revealing themselves in brand-new mediæval tights of purple silk, and short green doublets of a stuff they called "sanitæ." At this sudden sight, Mrs. Spratts' dormant sense of humour was at last aroused, and she poured forth such peals upon peals of laughter, that these unhappy men were offended beyond all hopes of reconciliation, and dragging on their every-day reach-me-downs in great haste, they shook the dust off their feet on the door-step, and left that hospitable house, never to return there again!

This incident led to the first misunderstanding that had ever occurred between Jack Spratt and his wife. He upbraided her with the loss of his old friends; whereupon she told him that it was no loss at all, and that they were a "duffing lot"—an expression she must have heard at Hurlingham, or on the baronial box-seat.

And Mr. and Mrs. Jack Spratt, who had been so closely united in thought, feeling, and sympathy, or, rather, who had always been as perfect complements to each other, each completing the other's being through harmonious dissimilarity of taste as thoroughly as did their thrice happy namesakes in the undying nursery rhyme, and like them reaching a common goal by apparently divergent ways, were no longer one and indivisible evermore.

Part 3.

MRS. SPRATT had not only learnt how to dress fashionably, and to laugh at the peculiarities of old and trusty friends, and to use vulgar, modern, slang expressions that would have made the fastidious Chaucer turn in his grave; but she had also learnt how to get rid of that unconsciousness which had once been as a sweet frame to her beauty, and which had so nobly stood the test of those little round mirrors in her husband's studio.

(Have our Lady readers ever contemplated themselves in one of these?)

During the early days of her married life she had often sat by her husband in the National Gallery, reading aloud to him, as he copied those singularly seductive types of female loveliness which the early Italian Masters have made so especially their own; and she had shared in his enthusiasm for them, and had often blamed herself for being so utterly unlike.

There had been one picture in particular, the *Martyrdom of Cupid*, by Luca Signorelli, in which Cupid himself, and the nymphs who persecute him, are of a beauty so overpowering that J. Spratt and the trusty friends would always feel faint, and weak in their backs and legs, through sheer excess of sensuous pleasure when they gazed at it; and varied as those nymphs were in form, hue, and feature, she could not claim the remotest resemblance to any single nymph amongst them, not even when she tried in a little round mirror.

Jack Spratt himself, who had fallen in love, courted and married before he had ever seen an old picture, could not but also feel at

YE ÆSTHETIC YOUNG GENIUSES.

times that his wife was not quite such as the early Italian Masters would have chosen for a model; and he had been confirmed in this

impression by the careless remarks of his trusty friends, who had not yet gotten themselves wives of their own (and who, although they would speak of *each other's* faces as "beautiful," "lovely," "divine," and so forth, were extremely fastidious in the matter of modern female beauty).

This disenchantment had been the one slight drawback to a happiness nearly perfect; but he had always been too much of a Gentleman to reproach his wife with her physical shortcomings; and had found both his consolation and his reward in her gentleness, her gratitude, her admiration for his genius, and her complete devotion to himself.

Moreover, although he could not alter her form, features, and complexion, he had endeavoured to teach her most of the early Italian attitudes, and she had proved a docile and intelligent pupil.

But now all this was changed; for wherever she went she was greeted with an admiration sufficient to turn an older and wiser head than hers; Dukes, Bishops, Generals, Admirals, even Right Honourables vied with each other in paying pretty compliments to the pretty Mrs. Spratt; so that she grew somewhat vain, and almost seemed at times as though she were half inclined to give herself airs; for instance, she would innocently blurt out before the wives and daughters of these great dignitaries (especially if they happened to be rather plain) that she would sooner be dead than not be beautiful, and the wives and daughters did not always relish these egotistical bursts of confidence.

Then there were the Royal Academicians, who also vied with each other in spoiling her; the painters painted her, one and all; and the sculptors sculpted, and the engravers engraved; while the cantankerous architects looked on with smothered envy; and gay young Associates, fellows of infinite jest, enlivened the sittings with inimitable song, dance, and story.

Not content with painting her, one famous artist, possessed of wide and varied information, and quite an authority in such matters,

solemnly stated that so beautiful a woman as Mrs. John Spratt had not been seen for four hundred years!

It requires less than this to make a pretty woman THE FASHION—which Mrs. Spratt immediately became.

So that even that lily of lilies, born of the foam of the sea, wafted hither from the Channel Isles by soft propitious winds, immortalised by Millais and Poynter, and enshrined for ever (along with a good many others) in the constant but capacious heart of Mr. Punch, was fain to abdicate from her throne in favour of that rose of roses, Mrs. Jack Spratt; and, to her inexpressible relief, was permitted once more to mingle with the gay and fashionable throng without attracting more notice than any other handsome and well-dressed lady; and as handsome and well-dressed ladies are by no means the exception in this gifted land, she had a nice easy time of it; quite a holiday, so to speak.

Not only the Fine Arts, as represented by the Royal Academy, but poetry, literature, and the exact sciences followed suit, and paid homage to the popular Mrs. Spratt in the persons of their most famous representatives—shining lights, whose names are household words all over the habitable globe; and such homage she would receive at first with gracious condescension, for she made it her queenly boast that she honoured true genius irrespective of birth or breeding; which was very good of her, for in her inmost heart she thought but lightly of these immortals who had worked so hard for their immortality.

It must be remembered that Mrs. Spratt had lived on terms of daily and familiar intercourse with the greatest geniuses of the age; for such, as she had always been given to understand, were her husband and the trusty friends; and this on their own authority; and these were, of all people, in a position to speak of such matters, being, as we have already said, critics as well as everything else, and knowing each other well.

There was Peter Leonardo Pye, for instance, the author of *Dank Kisses from Mildewed Lips*, who was quite the greatest poet that had

68

sung since Milton, as had been ungrudgingly acknowledged by Jack Spratt and the trusty friends, and even admitted by himself; though not without reluctance, for he was the very soul of modesty, was young Pye.

Indeed, so high were his aspirations, that he passionately longed not to be recognised by the world for many generations to come, and lived in constant dread of sudden popularity—thereby standing on a far higher pinnacle than any of the geniuses Mrs. Spratt met in Society.

Well, P. L. Pye wore side-spring boots, an æsthetic neck-tie, and trousers that would have been thought ill-conditioned in the Hampstead Road.

Burning thoughts, fiery though Platonic passions, and a habit of too recklessly consuming the midnight oil had wasted his once comely cheeks, contracted his chest, and made his shoulders round and sloping, and his legs so weak that he stood over like an old cab-horse; and proud as Lucifer though he was, and highly educated, for he had graduated with honours at the London University, he was only the son of a hatter; with whom he had, however, quarrelled and parted (which may, perhaps, have accounted for his always wearing such shocking bad hats); and his thoughts were so lofty and sorrowful that he kept most of them to himself, and those less lofty ones he had occasionally imparted to Mrs. Spratt had still been too lofty for her to understand, and had made her feel very uncomfortable.

And though he thought her quite the most beautiful woman he had ever seen out of an old picture (he never looked at any others), his admiration was expressed in such an abstract way that she could scarcely apprehend it.

So that she felt not only that Pye's company gave her no pleasure, but that to be seen riding, driving, or waltzing with him, even had he been capable of such accomplishments, would not have made her an object of envy in the eyes of other women; and it was the same with the rest of the trusty friends, who in genius, sorrow,

Ye GORGEOUS YOUNG SWELLS.

and shabbiness of outward form quite equalled Pye, if they did not indeed surpass him.

Whence she somewhat hastily concluded, that geniuses were careless in dress, eccentric in manner, very much taken up with themselves, and connected in some way or other with business; and she divided Society into two portions, those who were in Burke,

Debrett & Co., and those who were out of it, and looked upon all the latter as though they had been meritorious and more or less gifted hatters, worthy of all respect, but whose attentions conferred no social distinction on a pretty woman.

Argal, she much preferred the gorgeous gilded glittering swells who had been born to Swelldom, as she had been born to Beauty, without any fuss or bother.

For Swelldom is like the rose, in that some of its scent will cling to those who live with it; so, at least, thought Mrs. Spratt.

And Swelldom is pretty to look at, and wears trousers that never bag at the knees, and boots and shoes that do not turn up at the toes, nor flatten under the sole of the foot; and the flowers in its buttonholes are poems, and its hats, neckties, and gloves are always new, and always the very best of their kind.

Swelldom is friends with horses and dogs, and guns and fishing-rods, which are easier to master than pictures and poems, and the intellectual problems of the day, and do not wrinkle the brow, nor waste the cheek, nor sap the youthful frame; and its easy flow of talk is generally suited to the capacity of the greatest number, and its golden silence does not proceed from unpleasantly lofty speculation.

Nor is there anything at all abstract about that kind of worship which male Swelldom of whatever age will always render (unless duly checked) to lovely woman wherever it meets her; especially when her sole and exclusive claim to its warm regard lies in the exuberance of her purely physical charms; as was the case with Mrs. Jack Spratt, who had neither rank, wealth, accomplishments, conversation, nor repartee, and couldn't even say Bob! to her husband.

No, Gentle Reader, it was not Pallas Athene they worshipped in Mrs. Spratt, these gorgeous, gilded, glittering Swells, nor Diana, the chaste huntress of the silver bow, nor any one of the Nine Muses; but Venus Aphrodite, the goddess of visible, tangible love, whose apparent incarnation in Mrs. Spratt's beautiful face, smooth white skin, and ripely-rounded form they openly adored, with an adoration which Mr. Punch will describe as "concrete," in opposition to that "abstract" kind of adoration indulged in by Peter Leonardo Pye, and which Mrs. Spratt thought so vague, uninteresting, and slow.

And it speaks worlds for her guilelessness and purity that she should have accepted this wholesale tribute of concrete masculine incense as frankly as it was offered, and been honestly proud of the same, and looked upon it as conferring social dignity on herself, and honour and glory on her husband.

A more worldly and suspicious nature would have taken umbrage at once, and run away with the unhappy idea that homage of this kind, openly addressed to a wife and a mother, was but an insult in disguise, involving moral degradation instead of social dignity, and instead of honour and glory, only ridicule and contempt.

So that it was an unmixed pride and joy to her, wherever she went, to be surrounded by a crowd of smart male devotees, young and old, in whose tender tones of voice, and eager eyes observant of every detail of her face and form, she could hear and see unmistakeable evidence of a fervour as impassioned as it was direct and sincere.

But this manly devotion to Mrs. Spratt was by no means a source of unmixed pride and joy to the wives and daughters, who, to mark their disapprobation, not only ridiculed that Lady, and every peculiarity of her dress, gait, and manner, but actually imitated these peculiarities in their own persons, wearing their hair, moving and laughing exactly as Mrs. Spratt did; and all this whether they were young or old, tall or short, dark or fair, lean or fat—and so did the sisters, and the cousins, and the aunts.

Which gave boundless gratification to Mrs. Spratt.

Part 4.

JACK SPRATT, equally pure and guileless, and glad, as most of us are, to find his own taste justified in his own eyes by the good opinion of the world, began to feel an honest pride in his wife's beauty such as he had never quite felt before; and would not have changed her now for any blessed saint, virgin, or martyr in the whole National Gallery.

The truth is, that he had ceased to reverence those classic types.

For his artistic nature was quick to receive new impressions and to forget old ones; and with that tendency to generalise hastily which is so characteristic of youth, he would now state everywhere, on his own authority as a painter, that there was no beauty out of the English aristocracy, amongst whom he naturally included Mrs. Spratt and himself.

Moreover, it gratified his unselfish disposition to think that, after all, it was not entirely for *his* sake that Society had given so warm a welcome to *her*.

All of which did equal credit to his head and to his heart.

A more commonplace nature might have felt some jealousy; but Jack Spratt, who knew that he had within him all the jealous potentialities of an Othello, should any real cause for jealousy arise, could scarcely so insult his wife's good sense as to suppose that any of these amiable but mindless triflers who pestered her with their well-meant attentions, could ever be possible rivals for such an one as he.

These were indeed halcyon days!

Mrs. Spratt, as we have seen, by a burst of laughter so opportune that it might almost be called a stroke of genius, had cleared the house of the trusty, but not very presentable, old friends, and Jack had ceased to miss them.

The only surviving relative of the Spratts was Jack's grandfather, who kept an old established emporium for hosiery in St. Mary Axe; a good-natured and affectionate old man, who loved Jack with all a grandfather's partiality, but who had been much disgusted at his taking to such a beggarly and disreputable trade as painting pictures for hire.

If it had only been house painting, he could have understood it! However, as Jack was in independent circumstances, there was no gainsaying his right to choose his own line of life, and daub away as much as he liked; and the old Gentleman had swallowed his disgust, and would often drop in of an evening at his grandson's house.

These visits were not so pleasant to Mrs. Spratt as the old Gentleman believed.

Although circumstances had made him a well-to-do and contented hosier, Nature had intended him for a low comedian, or "funny" man; and he was never happy unless he made himself the life and soul of the party wherever he went.

He had never tired of poking fun at the trusty friends, for instance, whose lofty aims he could not sympathise with, and whom he had looked upon as a set of weak-minded, unwholesome, and affected nincompoops, and would mimic to the life under their very noses; especially Peter Leonardo Pye.

Now Mrs. Spratt hated fun, and thought it vulgar, as no doubt it very often is; and as for the trusty friends, they had loathed

"*Jack Spratt appeared on the scene.*"

Sprat Senior with deep though silent intensity, instead of doating on him as he had fondly imagined they did.

When Jack Spratt had become famous through the *Playre Sockyne-darrriere*, Spratt Senior suddenly viewed picture-painting in quite a new light, and became as proud of his always beloved grandson, as he had hitherto been ashamed of him; and he took to visiting at the Jack Spratts' regularly on Wednesday afternoons, Mrs. Spratt's day "at home"; but his visits were more unwelcome to that lady than ever.

At first the rank and fashion he met there awed him into silence and discreet behaviour; he had never seen a live lord before, for Swelldom does not usually buy its drawers and socks in St. Mary Axe.

And when he held his tongue and did not play the fool, he was rather ornamental than otherwise, being of truly venerable aspect, and scrupulously neat about his person.

But as soon as he discovered how easy and unconventional really good Society can be, how familiarly the glittering Swells would treat Mrs. Spratt, and how unceremoniously they would bear themselves towards that great genius, her husband (for they had forgotten by this time that he was a great genius, and looked upon him as a fool, or something worse), the irrepressible old humorist recovered his wonted assurance, and became once more the life and soul of the party.

It must be owned that his behaviour was very trying, and betrayed a great deficiency in social tact.

For instance he would, unasked, insist on favouring the company with long-forgotten comic songs (which had lost all point for the present generation), and imitations of the actors of a hundred years ago; and the less Mrs. Spratt and her guests would laugh, the more he would laugh himself, and the more he would persevere in trying to merit their applause by further efforts in the same line.

Then he would chaff the page who brought in the tea, and inquire of him if Sally the Cook were as good-looking as ever, and still reciprocated his fond affection.

Or else he would hand his business cards to Viscounts and Guardsmen, and ask fine Ladies where they bought their hose, and volunteer to serve them with a superior article at Civil Service prices, to be delivered at their own doors, carriage paid, and so forth.

At last a day came when he went just a little too far.

The Duke of Pentonville was at Mrs. Spratt's, alone; for so stupendous were his Grace's rank and fashion, so advanced his age, and so respected his character, that it was thought good form for Viscounts and Guardsmen and such like humble swells to make themselves scarce when *he* came—nor did they presume to knock at Mrs. Spratt's door when the Pentonville liveries were seen to be waiting outside.

Jack's Grandfather, who was quite wanting in this particular kind of delicacy, knocked at Mrs. Spratt's door without the slightest diffidence, and entered the house, and walked straight into the drawing-room after the fashion of Liston, in *Paul Pry*, exclaiming, " I hope I don't intrude ! "

The Duke stared at him with cold surprise, and immediately rose to take his leave. As he stooped, with old-fashioned courtesy, to kiss Mrs. Spratt's lily-white hand (into which he had just forced a costly trinket), the tail-pockets of his well-fitting green cut-away coat were seen to gape, and Mr. Spratt Senior took the opportunity of dropping into each of those ducal receptacles a printed circular, which stated that, owing to the sudden break-up of a well-known West-End Firm, Spratt & Co. had been able to effect extensive purchases in underclothing at an extraordinary advantage, which enabled them to supply the Nobility, Gentry, and Public generally with first-rate articles at an unprecedented low rate—a handsome discount allowed for cash.

Jack Spratt appeared on the scene as soon as he heard his Grandfather's voice, but it was too late to interfere; and the unconscious Duke, though much huffed at the untimely interruption, left the room with all the stately ease and high-bred self-control of a great

British nobleman of the old school, ignoring alike old Spratt's respectful obeisances, and young Spratt's friendly and familiar farewell; while the ends of the two printed circulars stuck symmetrically out.

Buttons, who admired old Spratt more than anybody else in the world, fairly exploded at this piece of practical fun.

But Mrs. Spratt could contain herself no longer, and gave her Grandfather-in-law such a piece of her mind as at last enlightened him about the estimation in which she and her Swell friends held his powers of entertaining the company; so that he left the house bewildered and aghast, with tears in his poor old eyes, and all the jokes crushed out of his facetious old heart for many a long day to come.

Nor did he ever cross that threshold again, much to the grief of the twins, who, although æsthetically reared, could not help adoring their mirthful and indulgent old Great-Grandpapa, who made them laugh so.

And to Jack's grief also, for he had a warm heart, and was tenderly attached to the old man, in spite of his "larks."

But in the exciting whirl of his new life, in which the days flew by like hours, a very few hours sufficed to obliterate these fond regrets.

And Jack Spratt felt no little elation in the thought that all their associates, however frivolous, were at least "Ladies and Gentlemen," a term which was constantly on his lips at this time, and which he only applied to those who were alike well-born, fashionably dressed, highly connected, and "in Society."

And now that Mrs. Spratt had so effectually disposed of that inconvenient old Grandfather of his, he considered himself as good as any of them; and bore himself accordingly; being politely distant to his inferiors, affable to recognised merit of a high order, free and easy with his equals, the Swells, and acknowledging no superior under Royalty.

Part 5.

BUT, in spite of the honour and glory, Jack Spratt found out, after a while, that he did not relish fashionable society with quite so keen a zest as at first.

He could neither dance, nor flirt, nor play cards. Of sport, the turf, and politics he knew nothing whatever, and cared as little for such topics as the gorgeous gilded glittering Swells cared for old music, old poets, and old pictures, which were his favourite themes, and on which he would descant most eloquently, and at great length, if anybody gave him a chance. The G. G. G. Swells never gave him a chance if they could help it, good-natured as they generally are. And it was borne upon him, in due time, that the illustrious representatives of Science, Literature, and Art did not come into the hollow world to talk or listen to the likes of him, nor even to each other, for the matter of that, but to practise repartee with noble Lords, and to instruct and amuse fine Ladies, which is capital good fun.

Jack Spratt had no repartee, and loathed fun; and although he could talk to fine Ladies with eager fluency, his talk was all instruction and no amusement, as the fine Ladies very soon found out; and for Ladies that were *not* fine he did not profess to care.

In addition to which, the more he saw of fashionable society the less he thought of it; for he not only met there Artists like himself, but caricaturists, and comic singers, and play-actors, and such-like folk, for whom he had an almost unbounded contempt; and these people seemed to get on better with the fine Ladies than he did.

So he got into a habit of hanging about, and standing in people's

"*Witching undulations.*"

way, and being jostled out of it, and would listlessly lean against walls and doors, and gaze by the hour at the mother of his twins (who used to think dancing so immodest), as she floated languidly by to the enervating measures of the Manolo Valse, rocked in the close embrace of some well-seasoned hero, of martial or diplomatic air, who never seemed to tire of his lovely burden; while her supple form, in its close-fitting sheeny sheath, would lend itself, as if by instinct, to all the witching undulations of the passionate "Lurch of Liverpool," or Boston's suggestive "dip."

Then rousing herself, as the strain would change, she would plunge headlong, supported by a fresh partner, into the stormy vortex of the polka, with a dishevelled recklessness even more seductive than her former dreamy and voluptuous *abandon*.

Or else in scented conservatories (discreetly dim), continental Princes with ardent exotic eyes, or foreign Ambassadors with tropical turns of speech, or polygamous Eastern potentates, with pearls and diamonds loose in their waistcoat pockets, would sit at her feet and ply her with the charm of their insidious conversation, while she fanned herself languidly, and drooped her sable lashes.

Or in the glare of crowded supper-rooms, bold, facetious Conservative Statesmen, or nice but naughty old Dukes, ribboned and starred and gartered so that there could be no mistake about them (which was always very pleasing to Mrs. Spratt—and small blame to her), would lounge over her alabaster shoulders, and whisper into her pretty little pink ear; they did not pour State secrets into that shell-like organ, but very straightforward compliments, or racy jokes, or risky little personal anecdotes about exalted houses, to the washing of whose family linen very few female Spratts are admitted in this nice, flattering, confidential way.

Fortunately, perhaps, absorbed as she now always was in the contemplation of her own peerless charms, she had contracted a habit of never listening to anecdotes of any kind, or jokes either; but she would reply to jokes, compliments, and risky little anecdotes alike with the same enchanting laugh that had more music than meaning in its ring; and this got the poor dear a reputation for being the reverse of prudish, which made her more popular than ever with the more elderly of her admirers; so that really clever, but rather plain women of the world, who made up for their want of beauty by their complete freedom from prudishness, were literally nowhere.

Mrs. Spratt's powers of conversation, never very brilliant, had been quite extinguished by her rise in the social scale. She was evidently made to be looked at—not to talk or listen. And yet, although there were many Ladies of high rank, quite as good to look at as she, and even more so, and who wore their dresses as low in the back, and as small in the waist, and as tight round the legs, and who, moreover, could both talk and listen delightfully to young or old, however frivolous, when it was worth their while; these were one and all deserted for Mrs. Spratt, and left to waste their fragrance on the desert air, and talk and listen to each other.

For not to be seen familiarly talking and listening to Mrs. Spratt, or rather pretending to do so, was to be "out of it."

And of all the men in that fashionable world, not one appeared more hopelessly "out of it" than Jack Spratt; and in all society there was nobody left for him to listen and talk to but himself.

Even *he* grew to perceive this in time!

He also grew to perceive that late hours interfere with work, and Mrs. Spratt had to go into the hollow world alone. Saddle-horses were brought round for her in the morning, broughams or victorias (according to the weather) in the afternoon, and in the evening there were dinners and dances, and bright little suppers in the small hours of the night, to which she could very well go without him.

For there was always at hand some smart unprejudiced woman of fashion, only too proud to *chaperone* the famous Mrs. Spratt, and who could keep always in sight, and out of hearing, and all that, just as well as the most innocently complacent of husbands.

"The same enchanting laugh."

He was not missed, and there was plenty for him to do at home, besides painting. There were the little red books of the butcher and baker to look after, and the lists to make out for the Civil Service Supply Association, and so forth; and then there were the twins. He had occasionally to take them out into the flowery meads himself—perambulator and all—and even sometimes to bath them at night, and teach them to say their prayers, and put them to bye-bye. For the nurse, a warm-hearted, but vain and extremely pretty woman in her humble way, was almost as fond of late hours and congenial society as her mistress, and much as she loved the pretty little darlings, who doated on her in return, she would sometimes yield to temptation, and leave them for gayer scenes.

They also doated, but in a distant and awestruck manner, on their mother, whom they very seldom saw, and then always in some new splendour of attire.

With unwashed faces and hands, in grimy little cotton frocks, and rice-milky bibs (everybody knows that the bib should be removed immediately after meals, and the pinafore resume its sway), they would patiently wait at the street-door, till they were rewarded by the sight of her, sweeping down the stairs and through the hall in her silks and muslins and laces; and before they could have said "Jack Spratt!" she was whisked away, telling them to be good, and kissing her daintily-gloved finger-tips to them, and showing her beautiful white teeth; and they would stare after her through the dust with wistful adoration.

Sometimes an organ would be playing a popular melody, such as "*Tommy, make room,*" or "*Don't make a noise*" (which are not so bad when you don't know the words), and, excited by the pretty tune, they would pretend that the dust was a golden cloud, and the brougham or victoria a fiery chariot, and their mother a being made up of a fairy, a queen, an angel, a saint, and a goddess, going straight off to heaven in a mist of glory; till the nurse would come and box their ears for standing in the draught, for her love was tempered with a wise severity.

At other times Viscounts and Guardsmen would call, and smoke their cigarettes in the pretty front parlour (Mrs. Spratt had never allowed the trusty friends to smoke when she was by, even in the open air); and the twins had to be kept out of sight, because they had holes in their socks, may be, and were not fit to be seen. And when the Guardsmen and Viscounts had taken their departure, and the little darlings hurried down-stairs to get a glimpse of their "lovely Mamma," she would tell them they were a perfect disgrace, and pack them off, crying, to bed; and quench the longings of her maternal heart by nursing a pair of Pugs, the gift of His Grace the Duke of Pentonville.

Female finery is very costly nowadays, and has to be paid for. Think of Jack Spratt, in the intervals of his domestic duties, painting against time, and wasting all that eagle-winged genius of his on pot-boilers, to pay for his wife's gorgeous apparel!

All his pictures represent pretty sock-darners, for it was the sock-darning and the pretty face, and nothing else, that had so touched the great heart of the British public in his first exhibited work; so he turns them out by the dozen in every variety of size, costume, attitude, and complexion. But the hired models he has to employ, got, have not the face and form of Mrs. Spratt; and all his sock-darners are inferior to that first one, and each sock-darner inferior to the last; so that a time must inevitably come when the great dealers will give him good advice instead of commissions, and finally cease to darken his doors, and he will have to darken theirs instead.

"A weary chase, a wasted hour!"

Be warned in time, ye rising young geniuses! Let no consideration tempt you into painting for filthy lucre, till you have realised a handsome independence by patient and steady devotion to Art for its own sweet sake!

Part 6.

MRS. SPRATT'S bed was not all roses neither. Smart people have at times a very provoking way with them. One day they are quite playful and familiar. The next, when we would be playful and familiar in our turn, with all the world looking on, they will publicly ignore us through a double eyeglass, to our great discomfiture, as we would naturally like to pass before the world for being their bosom friends.

That is, if we are Spratts.

And then they keep us in such tortures of suspense! either forgetting to bid us to the least our Spratty souls are hungering for, or else inviting us, as by an afterthought, at the eleventh hour, when we feel puzzled as to whether we had better be Sprattishly dignified, and decline with thanks, or put our prides in our pockets and go; and if we go, it is ten to one they will look as if they wondered what the deuce we are doing there; and if we don't, they never perceive our absence, and we are none the better in their eyes for the self-respect that has cost us so much self-denial. O we Spratts!

Also, it must be owned that Mrs. Spratt's beauty, and the very ample justice that was done to it both by herself and by the gorgeous Swells, did not greatly recommend that lady to the glittering Swellesses; so that she often met with cruel snubs and haunting slights from Ladies less beautiful, but of infinitely greater social importance than herself.

And she had not yet learnt how to dissemble when thus aggrieved, and swallow it all, and pretend she had not perceived it; nor could she yet toady the great of her own sex, and kiss the cruel hands that scratched her, and disarm such social tyranny by penitent, humble ways, without which arts no too pretty woman of her degree can appear to hold her own in the hollow world of fashion; nor had she, on the other hand, that mixture of thick-skinned impudence with ready mother-wit, which sometimes makes the merest *parvenue* a match for all the dowagers in England, and a thorn in their noble sides for ever; so that they give her a wide berth, and revenge themselves by telling each other that she is not a lady, and asking each other what they can expect.

Poor Mrs. Spratt! She couldn't very well put her tongue, and say "Yah!"

In after-moments of heartburning that came of such treatment, Mrs. Spratt would fold her children to her wounded bosom, and rail at the hollow world, and rave of love and peace and the homely domestic hearth, and the good old days of "Catscradle," and "Puss in the Corner," and the long-lost trusty friends, and the good old Great-Grandpapa; and, wildly calling for socks, she would darn them with any worsted that came to hand, the salt tears in her lovely eyes, a twin on each knee, and her clever Jack's protecting arm around her; and suddenly the postman would knock, and the Duchess's belated post-card arrive, just in time; and then, with jumps of joy, and trills of triumph, and a general scattering of socks, twins, worsted, and everything else to the four winds, upstairs to dress, and away, away to the hollow world again!

And there, such snubs as she met with, she would try to pass on to others; for even in the most exclusive saloons she would occasionally have to encounter people whose presence there was an offence to her. For instance, wives and daughters of Science, Literature, and Art; actresses of high repute; eminent female

physicians; great female philanthropists; poetesses, paintresses, authoresses, sculptoresses, and what not; worse than all, ladies whose only claim to distinction lay in their good looks and pretty manners.

Against all such upstart intruders of her own sex she would level her double eyeglass with happily copied impertinence. For just as those who rise from the ranks learn how to command by having first learnt how to obey, Mrs. Spratt had learnt how to snub by having been well and frequently snubbed herself. Fortunately for her victims, and unfortunately for her, she did not bear the Queen's commission, so to speak, and had no rank as yet beyond that which is conferred by the possession of a pretty face; so that her snubbings were of no account, and, consequently, recoiled on herself; for a premeditated snub which nobody feels, is almost as bad for its perpetrator as a premeditated joke that nobody laughs at.

Indeed, these harmless little airs and graces of Mrs. Spratt's were all set down to the fact that her late papa had been in the oil and Italian trade; which was very uncharitable and unjust, for they were only imitations of such airs and graces as she had seen many a real fine lady give herself any day; and very good imitations, too.

But one person may steal a horse, as we all know, while another must not even look at the stable-door.

And thus, snubbing and being snubbed, dressing and dancing and feasting and flirting, did she soar higher and higher in her butterfly career, and, in spite of the disadvantage of her oily origin, she achieved a social success which even transcended in its glory that of the better-born beauties, her predecessors on the throne of Fashion, whose features are so familiar to us all, and about whose doings, and careerings, and dressings, and so forth, we hear so much through the fashionable prints.

Indeed, all Mrs. Spratt's movements, where she went, what she wore, and how she looked in it, were duly chronicled for us week by week, and our mouths would water as we read how "Mrs. Spratt honoured a small-and-early at Marlborough House with her presence," or "was graciously pleased to attend the State Ball at Buckingham Palace," &c., &c., &c.

Her portraits appeared in all the illustrated papers down to the *Police News*, and were printed on pocket-handkerchiefs, and stamped on fusee-boxes and cigar cases, and cut out in gingerbread at country fairs; and her photographs, in every size, in every attitude, in every variety of dress and want of dress, were exhibited in the shop-windows, along with those of rival beauties of the world which has no English name. They were at all prices—from a shilling upwards; a reduction made on taking a quantity. So that even 'Arry, who is as partial to lovely woman as his betters, could afford to hang her up, framed and glazed, in his humble abode, and recreate his soul by the contemplation of her peerless charms through a magnifying glass, and descant thereon with his pals, and make comparisons, in his knowing way, between her and other beauties of his collection, and have a real good time.

And, in this particular instance, poor 'Arry showed rather to advantage, and was really more chivalrous, delicate, and romantic in his imaginary delectations than were the gorgeous, gilded, glittering Swells—possibly because he gazed on those peerless charms from below, as on some bright particular star.

But we will leave the erotic 'Arry, and return to Mrs. Spratt, who, wherever she went, was so mobbed that you might have taken her for an accident, or a row, or a fit, or a pickpocket caught in the act, instead of a pretty woman! She was even mobbed by titled crowds at royal and ducal garden-parties, where a couple of policemen were always retained to make a way for her to the strawberries-and-cream; and at State balls, dowager-peeresses would almost climb on to the backs of good-looking young actors to catch a glimpse of the beautiful Mrs. Spratt dancing with Royalty.

In vain she sought a refuge from this fashionable persecution in the solitudes of Rosherville, or the groves of Hampstead Heath

"Her portraits appeared at country fairs."

on a Bank holiday. Even there she was recognised (by our friend 'Arry, no doubt), and knock'emdowns, nigger minstrels and all, even the good old game of "kiss-in-the-ring," were deserted to stare at her (just as at Chiswick and Campden Hill; for human nature is the same everywhere).

When she appeared at the Opera, Patti sang in vain. In vain did our most fashionable preachers preach when Mrs. Spratt made one of the congregation; in vain did Messrs. Huxley or Tyndall lecture in Albemarle Street, or Professor Max Müller at Westminster Abbey, if Mrs. Spratt were among the lectured. Even the whales at the Aquarium would look small by Mrs. Spratt's side, and Cleopatra's Needle would lose its point if Mrs. Spratt drove on the Embankment. At the Crystal Palace people forgot to listen to the big organ; the cattle at the Cattle Show were left in peace; Irish Members obstructed Home Rulers; Mr. Gladstone lost the thread of his impeachment; Captain Shaw lost all control over his men; North London trains ran into Metropolitan; pleasure-vans drove, hooraying, into Marshall and Snelgrove's; steam-rollers rolled bang into Gunter's or Grange's; Old Bailey juries forgot to listen, Old Bailey judges to sum up, Old Bailey barristers were condemned to death, Old Bailey solicitors removed in the van, while murderers left the Court without a stain on their character; and Heaven knows what all besides! and all through Mrs. Spratt being there. Indeed, the only people who in that magic presence seemed to retain some self-possession, and keep an eye to business as well as an eye to beauty, were the pickpockets, who voted Mrs. Spratt a public benefactor; and the photographers, who blessed her very name!

And the best of it is, that everybody wondered how everybody else could be such a fool! especially the intelligent foreigner, who could not make out why, in this land of pretty women, there should be so much commotion about one pretty woman the more. And not such a very pretty woman either, he thought; for prettiness is a matter of taste, and not a mathematical certainty; and he would shrug his shoulders, and exclaim, "*Sont-ils drôles, ces Anglais, sont-ils drôles!*"

Part 7.

OW, Mr. Punch, who was kept *au fait* of all the Spratts' doings, and who had got to take a great interest in these young people, began to opine that their position was growing somewhat perilous, and that it was high time for him to interfere, like a *deus ex machinâ*, before another London Season should wax and wane, when it might perhaps be too late.

For dreadful things were beginning to be said about Mrs. Spratt; much too dreadful to be repeated here!

So he discovered, in the vernal glades of Camden Town, an American sculptor—one Pygmalion F. Minnow—whose wife was ever so much taller, plumper, redder, and whiter than Mrs. Spratt, and consequently twice as beautiful. So beautiful was she, in fact, that her husband had made a life-size statue of her, in illustration of Mr. Tennyson's beautiful poem, *The Mermaid*; and so beautiful was this statue, that the Royal Academicians found a place of honour for it all by itself (in the refreshment-room).

And so pleased were they by the singularly modest and unassuming demeanour of the sculptor, that, very much against his will, and although there was no vacancy in their ranks, they elected him full Royal Academician on the spot, a thing that had never been done at Burlington House before. Poor Jack Spratt!

Instigated by Mr. Punch, that plucky Baronet who had bought the *Little So-so-Dormir*, also bought *The Mermaid*, for his smoking-room; and not only that, but he gave the fortunate Artist a commission to execute from the same model a life-size statue of Diana, as she appeared to the enterprising but ill-fated Actæon a few moments before his untimely death; which work of Art was intended by this plucky Baronet to be a nice little surprise for his

good lady on her next birthday; and his good lady called on the sculptor and his wife at the studio, promiscuously, as she had done on the Spratts, and was so delighted with what she saw there, that she instantly dropped a fair Ethiopian ventriloquist, who could perform in five distinct South African dialects, and took up this young American couple instead, and invited them to a "small-and-early" at her house in Belgrave Square.

And there they had a success in the *tableau vivant* line that completely eclipsed that of the Spratts the year before, and the lovely Galatea Minnow became the fashion more suddenly, if possible, than Mrs. Spratt had done. And from that moment Mrs. Spratt might consider that her brief reign was over, and that she was for ever deposed from the throne of beauty.

Not that she abdicated without a struggle. The throne of beauty is wide enough for two, it seems; and two pretty women sitting close together, and thus publicly sunning themselves

"In the broad glare that beats upon a throne,"

make a much more edifying sight than only one. But the contest was soon decided in favour of the sculptor's wife. For although that omniscient Brother of the Brush (who had asserted that no such pretty woman as Mrs. Spratt had been seen for four hundred years) came forward with another assertion, namely, that Mrs. Spratt was *anatomically* finer than Mrs. Minnow, and would make a far more perfect skeleton, another lynx-eyed son of Apelles discovered that Mrs. Minnow's foot, although larger than Mrs. Spratt's, was constructed on truer artistic principles—more Greek, in fact; whereas Mrs. Spratt's, however fascinating to the Philistines, was rather Roman than Greek, and belonged to a later and somewhat degraded period of Art. So Mrs. Minnow, with her classical foot, won the day, and was the talk of Clubs and dinner parties throughout the length and breadth of the land; and Mrs. Spratt and her tootsicum were nowhere! *Sic transit gloria mundi!*

"*Le reine est mort! vive le reine!*" said his light-hearted old Grace

the Duke of Pentonville, who was very proud of his perfect French; and the *not*, coming from him, made quite a *furor*.

Jack was also destined to be unsuccessful this year. He had sent eight life-sized Sock-darners (with large landscape backgrounds) to the Royal Academy, with a short but perfectly polite note to the effect that he wished them to be hung all together in the large room, No. III., on the line, with sufficient space left between them to prevent their interfering with each other, and no other pictures hung above or below. There was also a postscript, mildly but firmly intimating that if these conditions were not complied with to the letter, he should feel bound for the future (in justice to himself) to exhibit his pictures in a private Gallery of his own, instead of sending them to the Royal Academy.

At the same time he displayed his tact by inviting the ten members of the Academy Council for the year to a banquet at Richmond, to meet two Viscounts, six Guardsmen, and an eminent Art-Critic. Previous engagements, it is true, prevented the ten Academicians from accepting this invitation; and as for the Art-Critic, he never even answered Jack's hospitable note. The Viscounts and Guardsmen alone accepted; but they never came.

So that the repast, though a sumptuous, was a lonely one.

Well, to his utter surprise and bitter mortification, the eight Sock-darners were rejected, without even so much as a line to explain why!

Nor would the dealers, great or small, have anything to do with those eight great Sock-darners; they had too many of Jack's wares on their hands already. Nor would the British Public; not at any price whatever.

To improve matters, and to pass the time, J. S. took to writing his views on Academicians, and dealers, and the British Public (and very strong views they were) in smart little pamphlets which he published at his own expense, and very liberally forwarded free of charge (and without previous application being made for the same).

84

But the worst was to come. Bad as it was in a financial and practical sense to be ignored by the Academicians, deserted by the British Public, and forsaken by the picture-dealers, there yet remained to Jack the gorgeous, gilded, glittering Swells, whose invitations last year had been so plentiful that he had occasionally revolted against them, exclaiming, "What nuisances they are, taking one from one's work, and running after a fellow like this!"

(For although smart people sometimes ask the husband without the wife, it would hardly do to ask the wife without the husband: only, Jack had never quite seen it in this light.)

But this year, strange to say, not a single invitation for the Spratts from any house really worth going to, was delivered either by hand or by post; and Mrs. Spratt would read aloud the fashionable arrangements for the week, and the week after, and the week after that; and not a card for any arrangement whatever, even at the eleventh hour! And even as she read, they groaned in the spirit together, and dropt the briny tear.

O ye Spratts! did you think it would go on for ever? Know ye not that all those wallowing sea-monsters of whom you small British fry are so dotingly fond, can be almost as fickle as yourselves—as ready to drop new friends for newer, as you are to drop old friends for *them*? Alas! pretty faces must not fade, pretty pictures never fail, and money be always forthcoming, for the likes of you to swim alongside of these giants of the main! And even if your power to amuse them *gratis* were perennial, and you were suffered to live among them to that end for ever and a day, you would still be only Spratts! And the porpoises would only roll over you, and the sharks tell you to get out of the way, for you are not worth eating up. Even the great good-natured Whales, whose eye and smile you live to catch, would hold out a fin one day, only to pass you by the next! And lord! how your fellow-Spratts would laugh when they heard of it all!

Had you but been a little less high and mighty, you might have commingled with another kind of fish, and not a low-class fish

either; and you might have grown in stature thereby, and even have acquired some of their flavour, and lost some of your own, a little of which goes a very long way! Are there not the herrings and the mackerel? the flounders, the plaice, and the soles? the expensive smelt, scarcely bigger than yourselves, but oh! how much nicer! the mullets, red and white, but especially red! the codfish, the turbot, the brill, and the salmon? And last, but not least, the delicate, nutritious, and easily-digested Punch? all of which live to useful ends, that they may feed and benefit mankind; and are the very salt of the sea!

O Spratts, be wise in your generation, an ye would be happy, and live out your little lives in undisturbed self-complacency and mutual admiration among just a few carefully-selected Spratts of your own size!

Indeed, for most of us work-a-day folk, whether we be of the Spratt, Sole, or Salmon tribe, what is there in all the Hollow World of Fashion really worth our stooping in the midst of our would-be betters? Truly and well sang the Augustan bard (we quote from memory):—

"Oh! quite too fortunate, did they but know
 Their own good luck, those Toilers, unto whom,
 Far from the madding crowd, kind Fate allots
 A red-brick house, well-stocked with china blue,
 And trusty friends, and twins: and, crowning all,
 *A lovely wife, whose beauty doth concern
 But one man only, and that man alone!*"

Part 8.

E will not follow Mrs. Spratt through all the steps of her downward social career, nor describe how she, who had seen Dukes, Ambassadors, and Princes at her feet, had for a time to condescend to grovelling Honourables, and fall back on Baronets again, and even put up with Knights from the City; how she rouged, and blanched, and violet-powdered, and blackened her under-lids, and auricoma'd and soda'd her beautiful black hair till half of it turned red, and the rest fell off; how she dressed more extravagantly than ever, and became extremely High Church, and sat in *tableaux vivants*, held stalls at fashionable bazaars, sang Offenbach and Lecocq at private theatricals, with short skirts on, &c., &c.

Even the Knights and Baronets failed her at last, and their dames ignored.

For some little while longer the *would-be* fashionable people—the hangers-on at the tail-end of Society, who had not yet received the straight tip about the sculptor's wife, or couldn't get her—would still ask Mrs. Spratt, in spite of the snubs she had showered on them the preceding year. And much as she sickened at the contact of their vulgarity—for what can be more vulgar than second or third-rate people of fashion?—she was glad of their countenance as long as it lasted. But even this was withdrawn in time, and she fell out of the hollow world of fashion altogether. The hollow world had grown sick of the Spratts, and dropped them—beauty, genius, sock-darning, and all!

And you may be sure that Poetical Justice was at hand, with scales inexorably poised, and sword on high! And heavily did she smite them as they fell; and thus ran her decrees:—

Firstly,—That John Spratt should become a bankrupt—which he did. And straightway that beautiful old red-brick dwelling, where they had lived since they were first married, and might have lived happily ever after, was placarded all over with unsightly bills, and defied from garret to basement by the muddy hoof of the ubiquitous Hebrew broker; and all their household gods were bared to the vulgar gaze; and every stick of their quaint old furniture was sold under the hammer, without reserve; and not a wrack was left behind to tell the wretched tale of ruin, except eight huge, frameless, staring Sock-darners, which nobody could be induced to buy, nor even take away for the sake of the canvas on which they were painted.

Secondly,—That the said John Spratt be written down a FOOL, so that his fame as such should reach the uttermost ends of the earth, and endure thereon so long as the English tongue be spoken.

"And think thyself lucky, thou miserable Spratt," exclaimed P. J. in her sternest accents, "that thy name should go down to endless posterity uncoupled with a still more disgraceful epithet!"

Thirdly, and lastly—(and here P. J. frowned ominously through the bandage that veils her impartial eyes)—That Mrs. John Spratt, wife of the above, and mother of his children—But what is this?

Oh! Woman, lovely Woman! ever since Troy became a heap of ashes (and even before!) what evil hast thou left unwrought, what wild and wicked things have not been done for thy sweet beauty's sake? And yet oh! to what base weakness hast thou brought the hearts of the sons of men, that even at the bare thought of thee crouching in shame and terror, and bathed in tears, the righteously indignant, but alas! too susceptible Punch should

87

falter in his just intent, and be foiled of his own set purpose at the eleventh hour!

For lo! he sinks him on his bended knee, and respectfully ventures to intercede on behalf of his most unhappy young friend, Mrs. John Spratt; he pleads her youth, her inexperience, the blindness of a silly, fatuous husband, the glittering baits and lures of a heartless, hollow world. He furthermore points out that the natural consequences of such a career as hers, if duly set forth, would quite too awfully harrow his gentle readers' feelings, and might very possibly, moreover, prove unfit for publication in his light and innocent page!

And behold! the generous plea prevails, and Poetical Justice, that greatest of all the Great Unpaid, tempers herself with mercy, and "sheathes her flaming brand!"

*   *   *   *   *

The Spratts are now comfortably settled at Acacia Lodge, a trim, well-built modern suburban residence, semi-detached, with gas and water laid on, Tobin's ventilators, Morris's papers, bath-room, scullery, lawn, summer-house, and all the latest improvements!

Truly, our heaviest troubles are often more than we generally do. At all events, Jack's failure proved a very good friend to Jack; for it not only brought home to him, before it was too late, the fact that he was no genius, and that his early success had been a fluke, and that his twopenny-halfpenny Art was but "the milder echo of an echo mild;" but it also brought his grandfather to his side again, and the fatted calf was killed, and the reconciliation complete.

Now, this facetious old Philistine, who was over ninety, had taken it into his head that his was a critical time of life, and that he required, for a few years at least, some rest from the cares of his trade; and it was arranged that the emporium in St. Mary Axe (a very genteel and snug little business) should be managed by Jack, whose property it would eventually become; and that Spratt Senior should spend the remainder of his days in peace under the same roof as his grand- and great-grandchildren, and be the object of their loving care as long as it should please Heaven to spare him.

Mrs. Spratt, a wiser, if not a sadder woman, is once more the brightest ornament of her home; her locks have grown again in all their sable splendour, the roses and lilies are blooming once more in her cheeks, and she is as plump and hearty as when she used to darn the family socks, ever so many months ago. It is once more to darn the family socks (she says) that she has given up the hollow world; but this must be taken figuratively, for there is always an unlimited supply of those useful articles from St. Mary Axe.

She has exchanged her spinning-wheel for a sewing-machine, and her skipping-rope for a lawn-tennis racket, which she plies with unerring grace and precision. And if she still reads the old tales of chivalry aloud, it is only for the benefit of the twins, who are just rising five, and therefore of an age most keenly to appreciate those beautiful legends.

She dresses just like any of her neighbours, only better, and her stately beauty is much admired. Indeed, when she walks (no longer mobbed) with her ruddy children (no longer quaint and old-fashioned) in the Zoological Gardens, and Spratt Senior, that nice, clean, respectable old gentleman, leaning on her arm, they form a picture of English middle-class domestic felicity which it does the intelligent foreigner good to see.

She never alludes to the hollow world but to speak of the folly of its men and the vanity of its women in terms of scorn and detestation, untinged, let us hope, with either envy or regret; and if she *does* take in the fashionable prints, it is only for the sake of their political opinions, and the graces of their literary style.

And she has always a bright smile for Jack when he comes home from business; and he is never without some elegant little article in the way of underclothing, bright-coloured and of delicate texture, either for the twins or herself.

"She plies her racket with grace and precision."

Finally, she has returned to the simple faith of her forefathers, and worships at Eyre Chapel, near the "Ebenezer Arms."

And the trusty friends?

Well, they have come back to the arms of Spratt, as true and as trusty as ever, but in different guise.

Disguised at never finding a publisher, and to revenge himself on the world for its neglect, Peter Leonardo Pye has foresworn the Muse, and is now travelling for his father's firm. He has hardly as yet acquired that ready smartness so useful in such an occupation, but is much improved in health and appearance, dresses better, and, though somewhat reserved and dreamy, is not unpopular "on the road;" and Mr. Punch more than suspects that his facility for writing verse has been turned to account in certain widely-circulated panegyrics of Pye and Son's masculine head-gear, unequalled for taste, cheapness, and durability.

And so with the rest of these trusty friends; for they can get no churches to build, no editors to take their aesthetic essays, no publishers to print their poems. And, by some strange fatality, the doors of the Royal Academy, and of the Grosvenor Gallery, and, indeed, of all the Galleries, British or foreign (especially foreign), seem inexorably closed to their productions. And having been led thereby, and also by the persistent gnawing of their empty stomachs, to the conviction that it is ever the fate of genius to starve, while mediocrity battens on the fat of the land, they have very sensibly cut the Fine Arts, and taken to commercial pursuits instead; and they are doing uncommonly well.

They have also clipped their hair and beards, and they get their boots and clothes at first-rate West-End establishments, and their gloves and scarves at Spratt's (cost price), and their hats at Pye's.

And they can smoke their pipes and cigars, the rogues, and toss off their brandies and sodas, and their claret cups, and their pale dry sherries; and even roar at the endless buffooneries of Spratt Senior (whom they have learnt to love), in spite of the death of the grand Old Masters. And they are always welcome at Acacia Lodge as flowers in May, for whatever we may think of their genius, their unsophisticated hearts are fond and faithful, warm and true.

And who so fit to appreciate these qualities, and hold them dear and sacred, as those storm-tossed victims of the hollow world's caprice, Mr. and Mrs. Jack Spratt?

And now, virtuous Reader, having relieved thy anxiety as to the fate of that worthy but once misguided pair, and steered them safe and sound into such a haven of respectability as, surely, was never reached by such perilous straits before (and probably never will be again), Mr. Punch will leave this tale to work its own moral in thy thoughtful bosom, and bid thee farewell for the present; for he has other business on hand, seeing that the sculptor's wife is giving the sculptor, and the Duke of Pentonville, and eke the Duchess thereof, and a good many more people besides, a great deal of unnecessary trouble!

A Model Hero of Modern Romance.

READER, how shall I limn this man for you, when the very sun has failed to do him justice—when the first photographers of the day have been driven baffled into their *cameras obscuri*! How account for the fearful impression that Vavasour Brabazon de Vere made on all women who crossed his path, ending but too often in the madhouse and the grave! And yet he stands before me now as he stood then, in that crowded assembly where he first met the Honourable Lady Velvetina Tresilian—lounging *nonchalantly*, as was ever his wont, against the faded wall-flowers of that

exquisitely decorated *salle de bal*, breathing proud insolent defiance on one and all!

Few men could tell his age, nor his height, nor whither he came from, nor whence he went when he went away. . . . Wo, alas! to those who could! Few women knew the colour of his tawny eyes for the thick settled gloom that shrouded them like a pall; and those who did had long since expiated that fatal knowledge under slabs of moss-grown granite and pillars of broken marble, inscribed with a name, a date, and nothing more! . . . . Eyes full and heavily under-hung—bloodshot

with imperial Norman blood! who could forget them who had once shrivelled and laid bare their souls under the scapulary of their cold indifferent gaze? They had that strange quality peculiar to Paul Potter's portraits of the Flemish aristocracy, that seem to follow you whithersoever you move; all who had met Vavasour had felt the spell of this ubiquitous glance, which gave him a terrible vantage over the dwarfed heroes of modern fiction, whose gaze is limited to one object at a time. Well has it been said of him—

"The moon looks
On many brooks;
The brook sees but one moon!"

Cold, haughty, sarcastic, unbending to a fault, he never stooped—no, not even when he picked up a lady's fan, or laced his own faultless Balmoral boot.

His small taper white hand was the envy of every duchess who had been privileged to behold it ungloved, and had lived to rue the privilege—yet was it hard as thrice-tempered crystal adamant—yet could it have bent and twisted the chiselled features of the Theseus so that Michael Angelo Buonarotti could scarce have recognised his own handiwork—crushed the full bronze torso of the Florentine Venus out of all semblance to a human face!

But, oh, reader! his voice!! full, dry, mellow, rich in musical impossibilities, it intoxicated one like wine, and left one staggering and powerless to resist; he, who hated music, was well aware of the potency of this spell—for yes, reader, he hated music, little as he was wont to boast of this aversion; his towering intellect and haughty Norman ancestry left such innocuous pastimes to meaner men—for him the passionate strains of Verdi had no charm—yet was his very silence full of melody! Rich, scornful, cruel, imperial, vindictive, unrelenting melody; whose cadences had been the sarcophagus of many! It is told of him that once, at a royal *matinee musical*, a Princess, secure in the "divinity that beats upon a throne" had dared to banter him on his indifference to the art of Balfe and Beethoven; curling his lip till the *sangre azur* flowed freely, he rose to his full height, stalked to the platform where the petted Tenor of the day held his audience in thrall, tore the music from his hands, and taking up the *area* where the astonished Italian had left it off, he finished it in tones so suave and enervating, with so passionate a pathos that all there who heard, hung on his lips for ever and a day, and the rest became epileptic for the remainder of their lives. The luckless *virtuoso*, Signor Gusbertiartini, went home, and sickened, and died of that song!

Poetry, he despised. Yet full oft had he, blindfolded, with his gloved left hand written impromptu epics that would have smitten a Tennyson with the palsy of incompetency! Art he loathed, with a guardsman's loathing; yet who does not recollect that exquisite picture of Rimini and Francesco di Paola, which all London flocked to see—painted by him for a wager on the bare back of a buck-jumping blood-mare that Rarey had given up as intractable?

He who knew every living idiom down to its very finger-nails —he for whom every dead and decayed tongue had yielded up its fragrance—had long found out the vanity of all things. Every science had he mastered, but only to sound the emptiness thereof. What wonder that this man believed in nothing under the sun? Nay, denied even that two and two made four. 'Tis but justice to state that he denied they made anything else worth living for. In his utter negation of all things, he did not even believe in the well authenticated tales that had reached England of his own marvellous adventures in untrodden zones,

familiar to him as the smoking-room of the most exclusive London clubs. For had he not pressed with the slender arab-arch of his foot, nay microscopically scrutinised with his cold passionless glance, every cubic inch of our mother-earth from zenith to zodiac, from equinox to ecliptic? Now unarmed and alone, battling with the wild bull-elephant in Siberian forests, whose fossil tusks would crumble into dust beneath his iron grasp—anon, ere the sun had risen and set again o'er his triumph, tracking the white bear to its den in the fastnesses of the primaeval Mexican steppe—now drifting over vast unknown inland seas of the Himalaya in a hollowed out bamboo craft of his own construction—anon, vainly wooed in the low sweet guttural diphthongs of the Zend Avesta dialect by golden-haired Nautsch girls, whose dowry was a prince's ransom, or discoursing sweet nothings in fluent Semitic to solemn-eyed Ckpszavchian signoritas with great sad ears, and the thick-skinned patience of the Sphinx! Seven times had the Sepoy's scalping knife performed on him its revolting office, as he lay steeped in some wild *haschish* dream, in lone wildernesses and remote "waste places of the fern;" seven times had he risen, Phoenix-like, from his own sack-cloth and ashes, and blown the slumbering spark of vitality into a lurid flame, wreaking a fearful holocaust on the red-skinned bravos who had, in the short lived triumph of their bloody vendetta, dared to trifle with the tawny crest that fair hands, braceletted with the ducal straw-berry-leaf, had been proud to toy with! And yet he never alluded to these "hairbreadth 'scrapes," as he lounged on the ottoman at "Whites"; clad in snow-coloured seal-skin dressing-gown, 'broidered with intertwisted monograms of golden fleur-de-luce (one of many such, yet not the best by far)—now withering the aristocratic *habitués* with sarcasms that fell from his lips thick and cold as the snows of an Arcadian winter—

now scathing the menials of the establishment with scornful look and word; for in his high-born contempt of the "*oi polloi*," he was ever mindful of the difference between the proud blue blood that ran riot in his own Norman veins, and "The poached filth that floods the middle class."

Is it strange that such a man should set all laws at defiance, laws of honour, courtesy, social intercourse, perspective, religion, scientific inquiry?—nay, the very laws of digestion itself? For to his world-sated palate the oyster and the oyster-shell were as one and the same—the one yielded no joy, the other presented no difficulty.

His hate was ruinous to men, his love fatal to women, his indifference, deadly alike to all, whether they knew him or not!

Again and again, wo, wo to the women who crossed his path, be they widows or wives, matrons or maidens! Down they went on their knees before him, like threshed corn beneath the shears of the mower, to worship for awhile at the shrine of his cruel glance, and then—withered 'neath his insolent scorn, flung away into the dim irrevocable future, like a worn-out glove, a soiled scarf, a slipper down at heel—far beyond all appeal or hope of redress from *him!* for it is of such men that Tasso has written:—

"Ye who outreat him, leave all hope behind." . . . .

Every husband, every father, every brother, feared and loathed him as the incarnation of the Evil one—in their mean, narrow, tedious nauseating philosophy they held him as a perjured villain of the deepest dye, steeped in utterest infamy!

Perhaps his greatest charm in women's eyes was that he was never heard to boast of this. . . . .

Oh, reader, is it a marvel that the Tresilian,— "The flower of the west-end and all the world," could not restrain a wild yell of agonised rapture when he, who never bent, yet bent his gaze on her, and stooping for

CRICHTON!

once in his life, stamped a seething red-hot kiss on her hand which, soldering her bracelet to her wrist, seared her white flesh through the scented gauntlet to her very palm, and claimed her as his partner in the "Mabel Waltz!" . . .

www.ingramcontent.com/pod-product-compliance
Lightning Source LLC
Chambersburg PA
CBHW032226230426
43666CB00033B/1606